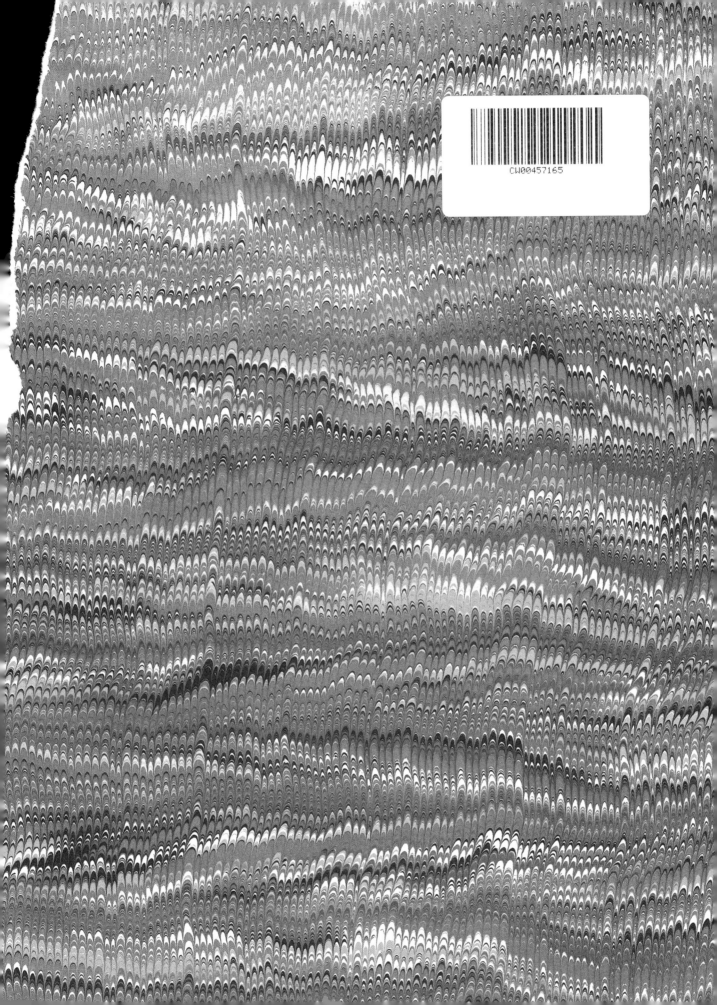

MILITARIA

Jan K. Kube

Prussia: Helmet eagle for enlisted men of Infantry Regiment 87, as of 1899.

Prussia: Helmet eagle for officers of the Home Guard, as of 1860.

MILITARIA

A Study of
German Helmets & Uniforms
1729-1918

Jan K. Kube

SCHIFFER MILITARY HISTORY
West Chester, PA

The photographs come from the authors archives.

Translated from the German by Dr. Edward Force,
Central Connecticut State University.

Printed in the United States of America.
ISBN: 0-88740-243-7

This book originally published under the title,
Militaria-Ein Bilderbuch für Sammler und Freunde
alter Helme und Uniformen,
by Podzun-Pallas Verlag, Friedberg 3 (Dorheim),
© 1987. ISBN: 3-7909-0304-3.

Published by Schiffer Publishing, Ltd.
1469 Morstein Road
West Chester, Pennsylvania 19380
Please write for a free catalog.
This book may be purchased from the publisher.
Please include $2.00 postage.
Try your bookstore first.

CONTENTS

1

1 Kaiser Wilhelm II in the uniform of an Imperial and Royal Austrian-Hungarian field marshal in parade form, 1902. Wilhelm II received this rank on May 4, 1900. Compare the color photograph of an original uniform on the dust jacket, which bears the insignia of a major general. The photograph is owned by the Huis Doorn Foundation.

This book was assembled for collectors and friends of historical uniforms and helmets. Its main feature is the photographic material, which will please the interested layman and the connoisseur alike.

Headgear, uniforms and pieces of equipment of the armies and military groups of the German kingdoms, grand duchies, duchies, counties, principalities and Hanseatic cities are shown, however, a complete survey is neither attempted nor possible. In naming the states, the status is not always clear, so the list at the end of the book is meant to help out in this respect. The size of the book did not allow inclusion of military items from foreign states, although many similarities can be found, especially in headgear, and could well be the subject of a future volume.

This book does not make any claim to being a scientific work. The bibliography included in the appendix is meant to provide a stimulus to further study and depth; and for those readers who are coming into contact with historic military items for the first time, it may be helpful to discover the incredibly wide range and cultural-historical significance of the realm of uniform lore.

For the most part, the photos and pictorial documents come from the author's archives, but at this point grateful thanks must be extended to the Huis Doorn Foundation of The Netherlands for granting permission to take and publish photographs of the uniform components of Kaiser Wilhelm II; to the Director of the Bavarian Army Museum in Ingolstadt, Dr. Ernst Aichner, for photos of Bavarian rarities; to Messrs. Peter Wacker and Gerd M. Schulz, as well as those collectors who wish to remain anonymous, who willingly allowed their treasures to be photographed.

Special thanks to my brother-in-law, Mr. Michael Kremnitz, who has tirelessly fulfilled my photographic wishes for the past fifteen years.

Thanks also to the publisher, Mr. Ahnert, of Podzun-Pallas Publishers in Friedberg, Hessen, for the publication and generous production of this book.

Sugenheim Castle, Summer 1987   Jan K. Kube

Prussia: caparison emblem of the Life Guard Cuirassier Regiment, 1902.

The term "Militaria" comes from Latin. "Res Militaria" means as much as "military matters", which is a general heading for anything military.

Today also, "Militaria" is a collective term for those things with which both the military scholar and the collector occupy themselves—be it the collecting of helmets, uniforms, equipment and other mementos of military history, or the study of past or present tactics, combat training, fortress construction or the history of formations or 'flags, to name only a few.

Even this brief list shows the many-faceted nature of involvement with militaria—specialization in one such area will be unavoidable if one is to achieve anything as a collector or historian. Two things were deliberately not mentioned above that may well apply but are not to be included in the concept of "Militaria": weapons and medals.

The collecting of weapons, especially of showpiece types, but also of war booty and thus the simple tools of the soldier, is a much older field of interest, pursued by emperors and kings, field marshals, officers and ordinary people within the limits of their means. It would burst the limits of this book to go into them, even in the narrowest terms of military ordnance. Then too, there are plenty of excellent publications about weapons of all kinds, whether defensive and protective types, military weapons or showpieces.

Medals and decorations cannot, of course, be separated from the subject of soldiers and warfare, but from the start they do not belong to the soldier's uniform or equipment, but are honors for extraordinary achievements in the realm of military activity. In addition, the subject of medals is not limited exclusively to war or soldiers, but has its roots in the realms of religion and everyday society. A medal or decoration of honor only belonged to a uniform when it was earned and thus commanded to be worn. The science of medals (phaleristics) is an independent science and only borders on that of uniforms. The collector of militaria will concern himself with medals chiefly for the purpose of decorating uniform jackets, particularly of the higher ranks, appropriately with medals and ribbons.

The history of the uniform, and military clothing, began around the middle of the 17th Century, with the introduction of regular armies or regiments that remained in service during peacetime. Until then, only mercenary armies were recruited for actual fighting, and were discharged again after the hostilities ended, and thus, naturally, had no tradition or relationship to a national army or people in any way. Only within the royal court troops were there old units that existed over centuries, such as the Royal Bavarian Life Guard Halberdiers, reliable details of whose history and uniforms were recorded as early as 1580.

The concept of a "uniform" comes from French (with Latin origins), and literally means "one form", thus uniformity within a large group. Naturally a 17th-Century uniform cannot be compared with an infantry guard unit's parade uniform of the early 20th Century. In the old days, "uniform" originally meant the existence of a uniform symbol, usually belts or armbands of the same color.

With the development of manufacturing and new dyeing techniques, it became possible at the beginning of the 18th Century to produce great numbers of identical uniforms. Of course the rulers in the early days of absolute monarchy saw the possibility of giving their troops the identifying marks of their flag or emblem colors, in order to express their power to command and create a loyalty—even if coerced—to the fatherland. The concept of the "commander-in-chief" was born in this era of absolutism; in the Thirty Years' War, which ended just half a century before, the field marshal or regimental commander still held the supreme command; an example of this is Wallenstein, who finally became too powerful as the Emperor's "gray eminence" and was assassinated at Eger in 1634.

Prussian Drum emblem, end of the 18th Century.

One can still make an impressive picture of an 18th-Century regiment, but certainly not in terms of their national unity, morale or even loyalty to their ruling prince. Desertions were the order of the day, and even in the Prussian army, regarded as a model in its day, there were numerous rogues, criminals and soldiers of fortune among the often forcibly enlisted ("recruited") soldiers, so that the officers could control their regiments only with Draconian regulations and punishments.

In the days of mercenary armies, officers and men were already known by varying titles of rank, and these terms have been maintained to the present with only minor changes. The common man was called a "Knecht" (as in "Landsknecht") for ages. This was not considered a derogatory term at all, and was related to the English word "knight." In the old days a Knecht was a servant, meaning a man who was in another's service. In time the old-fashioned term "Knecht" was lost and the "common man" (Gemeine) remained.

The German title of "Gefreite" (corporal) came from "Befreite", one who was free of standing guard, for guard duty was given only to reliable veterans. Thus this term in its original sense is not necessarily a flattering one.

"Unteroffizier" means one who is ranked directly under the officer. Higher officers were the "Hauptmann" (captain), the "Leutnant" (lieutenant) and the "Fähnrich" (ensign), while the lower officers provided liaison between the higher officers and the common soldiers, trained the privates and put the right man in the right place in battle. Veteran lower officers were usually promoted to "Feldwebel" (sergeant), for which there were appropriate positions in the regiments. This term originated from the word "Feld" (field) for the warriors as an entity (as in the term "Feldmarschall" (field marshal) or the term "field" as used in sports) and the verb "weiben" (weave), a concept taken from weaving, where the "Weibel" (the shuttle) rushed back and forth as quickly as a sergeant carrying orders.

The "Wachtmeister", another lower officer's rank corresponding to the "Feld-webel", was in charge of guarding and watching the army camp. The watches were generally handled by the cavalry, so that in the end this rank was reserved for the cavalry. The "Hauptmann" (captain) stood at the head of the company, thus being the leader of the smallest independent unit. His representative was the "Leutnant", from the French "Lieutenant" (French "lieu", place, and "tenir", to hold). In the cavalry the captains were known since olden times as "Rittmeister" (riding master). The "Fähnrich" (ensign) originally carried the flag; later the officers' assistants were generally known by this term (the "Degenfähnrich" could bear the officer's sword, the "Portépée-Fähnrich" could wear the officer's sword-belt).

Greater numbers of positions and enlargement of regiments, battalions and companies led to the creation of additional ranks for officers' "representatives", such as "Oberleutnant" (first lieutenant) and "Oberstleutnant" (lieutenant colonel).

The "Oberst" (colonel) was the highest-ranking captain, thus the commander of the regiment, which was divided into companies which all had captains (Hauptmänner), and the "Oberstleutnant" (lieutenant colonel) was his representative.

In addition to his direct representative, the colonel also had a sergeant directly under him, the "Oberst-Wachtmeister." This concept changed quite early, and the Spanish word "majór" (administrator, overseer) was used instead, creating the rank of "Major."

The ranks of generals can be explained similarly: first came the commanding general, then his "representatives", the "Generalleutnant" (lieutenant general) and his "Wachtmeister", the "Generalmajor" (major general). This explains why the lieutenant general outranks the major general, which is incomprehensible to the layman, since the major outranks the lieutenant.

In the "Old Army" before 1918, each major general commanded a brigade (which consisted of two regiments); a lieutenant general commanded a division (composed of two infantry, one cavalry and two field artillery brigades, their home-guard and reserve troops and special units such as engineers, supply trains etc.); each general commanded an army corps, which consisted of two divisions. The "Generaloberst" (literally "colonel general") was in charge of army inspection as an "inspector general", to whom three army corps were subordinate. The ranks of "Generaloberst with the rank of Generalfeldmarschall" and "Generalfeldmarschall" (field marshal) entailed the command of an army group, and the first title could also be used as an honorary title for a man of royal blood.

Special units and groups deviated from this system, as many documented exceptions to the rule prove.

During the course of the 18th Century, military dress became more uniform, not only in the army but also within individual regiments, and certain colors and details gave the regiments their own appearance. Success in combat brought the individual regiments special decorations such as sword-knots, stripes on their helmet emblems, special features of their uniforms or special privileges. One of these decorations, the "Cassano sword-knot" in memory of the Battle of Cassano on August 16, 1705, was last worn in the Prussian army by the 7th and 8th Companies of the Tsar Alexander Grenadier Guard Regiment No. 1, remained in use almost 250 years, as this mark of honor was still worn by the 3rd Company of Infantry Regiment 67 in the Wehrmacht until 1945. It has meanwhile been shown by military research that the Cassano origin cannot be correct, but in spite of that, the tradition, once accepted, was maintained.

This is surely a good example for other such cases. Nevertheless, tradition has been of great importance in military circles and has contributed to soldierly unity.

Kaiser Wilhelm II (reigned 1888-1918) had a special preference for the times of his ancestor Frederick the Great (1712-1786), and gave several of his regiments decorations that were meant to recall that glorious era, such as the grenadier caps of the 1st Guard Regiment (1894), the ring collars of the Gardes du Corps Regiment (1912), the Life Guard Cuirassier Regiment (1896) and the Queen's Cuirassier Regiment (1895), to name the most important.

Curious incidents also led to particular uniform details. Once Kaiser Wilhelm I, then very old, forgot to button the top button of his overcoat when visited by the officers of the Cuirassier Guard Regiment—and in order not to embarrass the august gentleman, all the officers quickly opened their top buttons as well. Thus an awkward situation was avoided and a special detail was born.

The identifying mark of the officer was the ring collar, a relic of knightly armor that had developed out of the neck protector and was finally worn as a half-moon emblem on a silk ribbon around the neck. These ring collars were handy, as the emblem of the ruling prince or regimental commander could be hung on them. This could be done more or less ornately, depending on one's financial means. Around his waist the officer wore a belt bearing the colors of his state.

Prussia: Banner of the Prince Louis Ferdinand of Prussia Infantry Regiment (2nd Magdeburg) No. 27, circa 1912.

Additional insignias of rank, especially those of officers, did not exist in the 18th Century. Only the officer's age gave any indication of his rank. The officer's most important badge of honor was the "port-épée", the sword-knot. Literally the "sword-carrier" in French, it originally served to link the sword firmly to the wrist to prevent it from being lost. Later it became only a sign of the officer and, for the cavalry, the "fighting troops", a hand strap with its original function; in the infantry it became a "saber band" or "sword-knot." From 1816 on, the different colors of these straps and knots were used to differentiate companies and squadrons.

Generals originally wore the uniform of their regiments. Only toward the end of the 18th Century did special generals' uniforms appear—at the beginning of the 19th Century they were generally specifically prescribed. The special features of Napoleon's generals' and marshals' uniforms were imitated by many a German general, but were kept within limits. Only the height of the general's hat became a particular fad, especially in the 1820's. Since the early days, officers had to provide their own clothing and equipment—until the 18th Century, a regimental commander often had to outfit, arm and support his entire regiment out of his own pocket. The men were not given free uniforms either, there were "economy regulations" and "outfit rate systems" by paying which pieces of military clothing gradually passed into the man's possession. Often the payments lasted longer than the piece of clothing. Somewhat after the middle of the 19th Century the free provision of uniforms to the enlisted started.

Bavaria: Buckle, end of the 18th Century.

The outfit rate systems worked well, though, especially as the previous practice of obtaining the enlisted men's uniforms from the colonels themselves set no limits on their extent and often drove the men farther into debt than was necessary.

Also, in the 18th Century, the colors of the larger states originated—colors such as Prussian blue, Russian green, English red, to name only a few, remained in use until the 20th century. The choice of colors was determined by the availability of the coloring material in the country itself. The smaller countries, not as strong financially, used uniforms that resembled those of the larger countries with which they were allied. Austrian uniforms were white until 1866, and so were those of Saxony, which was usually allied with Austria. Such a strict system of colors existed only in the infantry, though, while the cavalry, especially the hussars, wore much more colorful uniforms.

Baden: Artillery officer's cartouche box, circa 1830.

Of course a "white" uniform does not mean one made of a pure white woolen fabric. The fabrics of the 18th Century were notably crude and rough, more "natural color" than white, and the uniform itself was constantly coated with white paint or wet chalk ("gekollert", from the French "couleur", color: note too the origin of the Prussian cuirassiers' white "Koller"!) The optical impression of this treatment of the cloth was certainly not of the best, quite aside from other disadvantages such as the smell or the constant dripping of bits of paint. The only important thing was the impression of the troop as a whole, so that friend and foe could be told apart in battle. The muzzle-loading weapons of the 18th and 19th Centuries created such a fog during a battle that it was possible to tell the two sides apart only on the basis of color.

The uniforms of the 17th and the first half of the 18th Centuries had a very broad, almost comfortable cut. As the armies constantly grew, more and more new uniforms had to be made and delivered. Thus it can be ascribed not only to fashion but also to "Prussian" thriftiness that the uniform cut became increasingly tight and snug; it was commonplace for a soldier to jump off a table into his trousers, which a comrade held, for otherwise he would not get into them. But not only the cut and the color of the uniforms changed—the soldiers' headgear also went through constant changes.

With the further development of technology, uniforms could now be made of finer fabrics, but it was probably only the officers who profited by this development. The officers' desire for polish and decoration, which already drew criticism by the end of the 18th Century, hit its peak in the beginning of the "new era", as the individual ruling princes tried to master this style, and failed more or less. The enlisted man's uniform also took on a much better appearance and became more comfortable. Naturally, the monetary circumstances of the time often set limits to what was wanted.

The Wars of Liberation brought a totally new type of soldier. The soldiers were no longer kept in their regiments by iron discipline and punishment, for now the newly developed patriotic-sentimental enthusiasm inspired a hitherto unknown fighting spirit and morale in those lands that were suffering under Napoleon's rule. From

France there came a new symbol that united the soldiers: the cockade. The national cockade was introduced gradually to all the troops in the Prussian army after 1808, first only on the shako, and later on other headgear. To this day the cockade or rosette remains the most important, most unifying military emblem.

In the Napoleonic Era the uniform frock coat, which was customary until then, changed into the "Kollett", a trimly cut uniform with thin sleeves; it reached only to the waist, and its two tails in the back grew shorter and shorter over the years. The soldier's queue, that well-preserved and protected relic of the 18th Century, disappeared along with the frock coat. In 1807 the first parade of queueless guardsmen took place in Prussia, and inspired much opposition among the conservative officers' corps.

At the beginning of the 19th Century, insignias of rank were introduced in all countries, in order to make differences in rank clear and recognizable for everyone.

At the same time as the introduction of the "Pickelhaube" helmet in Prussia, the "Waffenrock" jacket also appeared, replacing the old-fashioned and impractical "Kollett." This new uniform jacket now had straight bottom seams, and became the clothing of the Prussian soldier—and almost all the world's other soldiers. The previous insignia, such as the guardsmen's patches of braid, epaulettes, braid and piping were applied to the uniform jacket. Other changes were made to the officers' shoulder pieces (first worn in 1866), as well as the introduction of the field belt and uniform belt, boots instead of laced shoes, new packs for enlisted men, and the constant testing of new equipment.

The long years of peace after 1870 brought no need for major changes in uniforms. Rather, the soldier felt comfortable in his handsome uniform, and found his justification in the esteem of his state, which ranked the military above all other levels of society.

The Boxer Rebellion in China in 1901 and the action of German troops in Africa resulted in serious consideration being given to the introducion of modern, practical uniforms, which were originally developed for tropic use, and finally resulted in the new "field gray" 1910 model uniform for the entire army back home. Superfluous parts such as epaulettes, parade trimmings like facings or useless pieces of equipment like bandoliers, saber scabbards or cuirasses were now removed from use in the field, but were retained as before for peacetime uniforms. Despite the new features, the field-gray uniform, still with its typical identifying marks of individual service arms, such as the service jacket with a single row of buttons for foot soldiers, the Ulanka for the Uhlans, the Attila for the Hussars, and the accompanying headgear such as the helmet, chapka, fur cap or cuirassier's helmet and shako, their colors varied only by helmet coverings, were as impractical for warfare as before. Still in all, the glittering buttons, gold and silver panels and braid, not to mention embroidery, had disappeared—there use had led to the loss of many officers in battle, as they could be seen from afar because of their shining insignia. Old uniform traditions were brought to new life, though, with the introduction of the so-called "future peacetime uniform." This new uniform, introduced in September of 1915, brought back colored collars and cuffs, silver or gold buttons and glittering embroidery for the guards, grenadiers and various other special units. To be sure, these field-gray but once again brightly decorated uniforms provided more glitter and glory than a camouflaged fatigue jacket. But since these new uniforms were supposed to be used only in future peacetime, their use remained optional, and so only comparatively few of these uniforms were made.

Originally, there was no connection between uniforms, their cut and equipment, and the headgear worn with them. For example, the Hussars changed from the fur cap to the peaked cap, then from the shako back to a modified fur cap, and then tried out the old shako again in Prussia (Life Guard Hussar Regiment 19, circa 1913), while the tied Attila remained for centuries. The Bavarian cuirassier lost his cuirass in 1873, used a leather helmet in 1879 that was modified in 1886, but kept his usual uniform coat. The Bavarian Jäger wore his "crested helmet" for decades, had a "Pickelhaube" for a short time (1886-1890), and finally received a Prussian-type shako—the uniform, however, did not change.

The connections between uniforms and civilian fashions are well known and need no further discussion here. The soldier's tendency to decorate himself with all possible feathers, furs and shining braids has been well researched and attributed to the awareness that the soldier needs to relate his social position, his air of importance and his activities with many examples from the world of animals.

Braunschweig: Officer's cartridge box of Hussar Regiment No. 17, circa 1912.

Historische Entwickelung der Uniformirung des 9. Infanterie-Regiments.

1) Musk. Uffizr v. Stamm-Rgt. Rodenhausen 1778-85.   2) Fusilier v. Rgt. Rodenhausen 1789-99.   3) 9. Inf.-Rgt. Gemeiner 1806.   4) 9. Inf.-Rgt. Oberlieutenant 1812-14.   5) 9. Inf.-Rgt. Gemeiner 1848.   6) 9. Inf.-Rgt. Gemeiner 1866.   7) 9. Inf.-Rgt. Gemeiner 1870.   8) 9. Inf.-Rgt. Gefreiter 1895.

2 Reprint from the "History of the Royal Bavarian 9th Infantry Regiment, Wrede", Würzburg 1895, showing the development of uniforms from the tailcoat via the Kollet to the service jacket, circa 1778 to 1895.

3

4

3 Prussia: Reprint from the, *History of the Tsar Alexander Grenadier Guard Regiment No. 1*, by A. Kries, Berlin 1889, showing the uniform tailcoat of the 18th Century, the Kollet of the Wars of Liberation and the service jacket worn from 1842 on.

4 Prussia: Reprint from the, *History of the Fusilier Guard Regiment, its Original Troops and Units*, by V. Asbrand, known as Porbeck, Berlin 1885, showing the development of headgear from the bombardier's cap to the shako in the years before 1842.

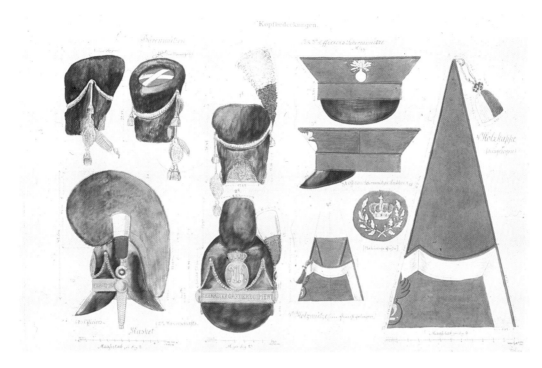

5

6

5 Bavaria: Reprint from, *The Royal Bavarian Grenadier Guard Regiment from 1814 to 1826*, by K. Müller and Th. Kurz, Munich 1900, showing the various types of headgear worn by a guard regiment, such as the service casquette, bearskin parade cap, pointed cap (also called the "wood cap") for enlisted men off duty (in camp, etc.) and the officer's peaked cap.

6 Saxony: Reprint from the, *History of the Royal Saxon Army*, by Dr. F. Hauthal, Dresden 1859; an example of the colorful, ornate uniforms of Hussars common throughout Germany.

24

25

24 Prussia: General's hat, 1806-1825, with gold star clasp (later fringe clasp), plus plumes and original cardboard box.

25 Bavaria: M/1825 general's hat, with blue and white rooster-feather plumes. Worn thus until 1873. Before 1825 the general's hat was even higher and decorated with a wide, patterned silver stripe. In Bavaria—unlike the other states—the trimmings of generals' uniforms and hats were made of silver.

44

44 Bavaria: Casquette ("Rumford Hat") for fusilier officers, 1789-1800. The formerly white plume of horsehair has darkened. The front brass has raised decoration and is fire-gilded. The helmet itself is made of pressed, lacquered felt, the brim of leather.

21

45

45 Casquette for light cavalry regimental officers, M/1818 (worn till 1825).

55

55 Bavaria: Officer's helmet and cuirass of the Garde du Corps, M/1814, fire-gilded brass, bearskin crest. This regiment, already planned in 1811, was founded only on July 16, 1814, and was disbanded on November 20, 1825 for the purpose of saving money in the military budget. The members of the regiment joined the 1st Prince Karl Cuirassier Regiment.

58

58 Bavaria: Officer's helmet for cuirassiers, M/1845, with bearskin crest, worn from 1845 to 1848 and again from 1864 to 1873. It is not possible to tell the helmets worn under King Ludwig I from those worn under Ludwig II, as their appearance and preparation were identical. Likewise the officer's cuirass M/1815 with original red cuff with silver embroidery; the officer's cuirass did not change its appearance and remained the same until 1873.

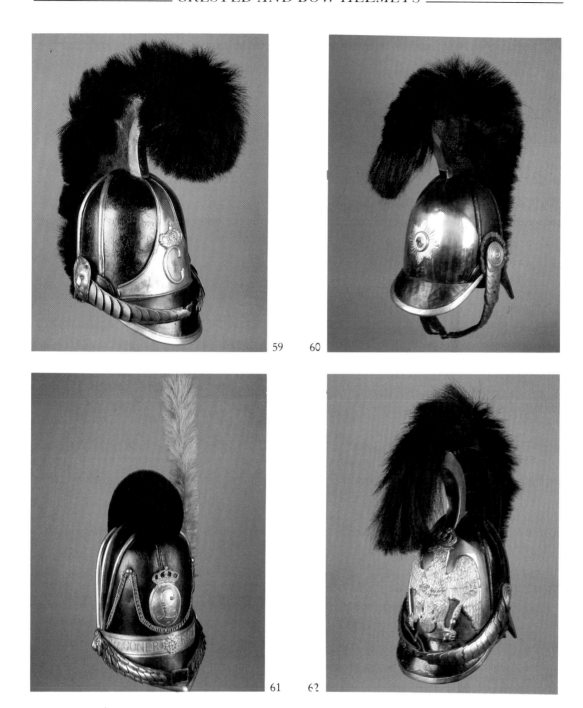

59   60

61   62

59 Baden: Enlisted men's helmet of the Dragoon Regiment of Freistedt, 1810 (worn until 1818). With the initial of Grand Duke Carl.

60 Prussia: Officer's helmet for the Gardes du Corps and Cuirassier Guards, M/1808, this version circa 1820.

61 Baden: Officer's helmet of the Light Dragoon Regiment, M/1808, this version first worn in 1818 (Grand Duke Ludwig I, who reigned until 1830).

62 Prussia: Cuirassier officer's helmet of the line regiments, worn from 1830 to 1842.

57

57 Hannover: Officer's helmet M/1816 for cuirassier guards, with the officer's cuirass. Worn until 1833, when the regiment was changed to dragoons and given leather bow helmets with horsehair crests.

56

56 Hannover: Officer's helmet and cuirass M/1815 for the Garde du Corps Regiment. Worn until 1833. The helmet is fire-gilded with massive silver trim, following the model introduced at the same time in England for officers of the 1st Life Guards.

63

64

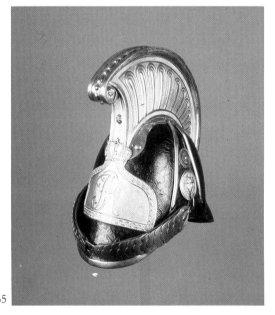
65

66

63 Baden: Helmet for dragoon officers, M/1834, worn until 1850. Variation of this model worn without horsehair crest.

64 Baden: Dragoon officer's helmet M/1834, as worn from 1848 to 1850, with federation cockade under that of the state; with horsehair crest.

65 Saxony: Enlisted men's helmet of the cavalry regiments, M/1849, version with the monogram of King Johann, since 1854. This model was worn without a crest. In 1867 a new, lower model with a crest was introduced.

66 Saxony: Officer's helmet of the cavalry regiments, M/1849, the 1854-1867 version.

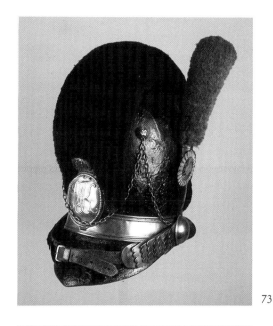

73

74

75

76

73 Bavaria: Casquette for the infantry, M/1808, worn until 1818. (After 1818 the service-arm emblem was placed on the previously smooth brass ring.)

74 Bavaria: Jäger helmet, M/1845, 1848 version. For the Jägers, the eye-catching, gleaming "sun" emblem was done away with, and only the initial "M" and the crown were used.

75 Bavaria: Artillery officer's helmet, 1861 model, as worn from 1864 to 1868, with red hair plume and brass trim on the sides.

76 Bavaria: Light cavalry officer's helmet, M/1868, with parade brush at the left, made of white ostrich feathers, in a diamond-shaped silver-blue socket. (The standing white horsehair plumes of the enlisted men were replaced in 1873 by hanging ones of the same material.)

248 Bavaria: Officer's helmet, M/1832, for light cavalry and artillery. The helmet, now considerably lower, offered lighter weight and a better seat on the head, especially while riding, without eliminating the trim used since 1808.

158

159

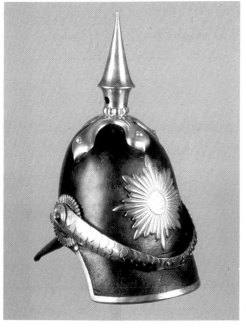

160

161

_158_ Schleswig-Holstein: Infantry officer's helmet, 1848-1850.

_159_ Lippe-Detmold: Infantry officer's helmet, 1848-1861.

_160_ Lauenburg: Officer's helmet of the Ducal Infantry Battalion, 1849.

_161_ Bremen: Officer's helmet of the Volunteer Infantry, 1850.

180

181

182

183

180 Prussia: General's helmet owned by Kaiser Wilhelm II, with parade plume.

181 Württemberg: General's helmet, post-1897, with parade feather plume.

182 Bavaria: Helmet for adjutants-general and surgeons-general, with enamel coat of arms as of 1913.

183 Oldenburg: Helmet for the grand duke's flank adjutants, circa 1912, with parade feather plume.

Since olden times the soldier's chief concern has been protecting his head. Discoveries of helmets from pre-Christian times prove this. The heavily armored knights disappeared with the dying Middle Ages, and the new fighting groups that appeared on the scene dispensed with unhandy iron armor and helmets by using different tactics. Between the Thirty Years' War and the end of the 17th Century, iron helmets disappeared and broad-brimmed hats were used. It remains to be determined why so little attention was given to protecting one's head then. It is definite that the first (mercenary) soldiers' hats worn in the 17th Century were no different from the civilians' normal headgear. There weren't hats designed especially for military purposes, nor was it possible to spend much money on outfitting mercenaries hired only for a short time. The broad-brimmed round hat that offered protection from wind and weather was generally worn.

With the beginning of purposeful uniforming around 1700 and the use of muzzle-loading guns, it became apparent that a broad-brimmed hat hindered a man's use of his gun. The brims were turned up, the tricorne came into being, and immediately entered civilian fashions as well. Musketeers (so called after their weapon, the musket) and fusiliers (from the French word "fusil", gun) wore these hats. The grenadiers (grenade throwers) were hindered by these hats when throwing, and so they were given the so-called "grenadier cap", a piece of headgear that developed out of the civilian "Zipfelmütze" cap, which had no brim. The point originally hung down in the back, but was later stiffened and worn vertically, so as to make the man look bigger. Pieces of metal decorated with lettering or symbols, or colorful embroidered cloth emblems, usually stiffened with cardboard and running to a point, were used on the front—the fringe of the ball finally became a ball at the top.

The grenadier cap has often been compared to the papal tiara, but this comparison does not hold water, particularly not on a religious basis. The motto "With God for King and Country" came into being a good century later, at the time of the Wars of Liberation against Napoleon.

Although grenade-throwing soon faded into the background of military science, the grenadiers retained their honorable name and later became the elite units of the infantry.

The fusilier's cap was introduced at about the same time as the grenadier's cap, though there does not seem to be any good reason for the difference, since the fusiliers were trained and applied exactly as the grenadiers were. Yet the crown of the fusilier's cap was not pointed, but round, and the shield was not connected to the crown. The fusilier's cap had no cloth ball, but rather a metal orb on top of the crown. The bombardiers of the artillery and the miners of the miners' corps (engineers) were also given similar caps, though of an even lower shape.

Along with the grenadier caps in all their variations, there were fur caps that originated in Eastern Europe. Here the pelts of bears, otters or other animals were used, and the caps were worn with or without metal shields on the front; some caps had a cloth panel ("mirror") on top, on which emblems such as an exploding grenade or a cross of braid were worn.

Yet these fur caps were not particularly popular, as they gave the soldiers particular trouble by falling prey to moths or beetles. So these caps fell out of general use and were reserved only for guard troops, such as the Bavarian Grenadier Guard Regiment established in 1814 (the later Infantry Life Guard Regiment), but as early as 1821 they were done away with completely, even before the whole regiment had been supplied with them. The Saxon Grenadier Guards, the Württemberg Foot Guard and the Guards of Saxe-Coburg also wore bearskin caps for only a short time. By the middle of the 19th Century there were bearskin caps only in the Hannover Guard Regiment for parade use, as well as in Mecklenburg-Schwerin, where they lasted until the end of the monarchy. The grenadiers of the Bavarian Home Guard kept their bearskin caps in individual cases until 1870, while in Hamburg they were worn by the carpenters of the Citizens' Militia until 1853.

Prussia: Embroidered star of the Order of the Black Eagle (guard emblem) for officers' caparisons, circa 1870.

In general, the grenadier caps went out of use toward the end of the 18th Century, as in Prussia when King Friedrich Wilhelm II came to the throne in 1786 and replaced them with two-lapped hats. King Friedrich Wilhelm III (1797-1840), though, introduced a new type of grenadier cap in Prussia in 1799—these consisted of a shield edged with bearskin, with a projecting black Prussian eagle and a peak in front. After the disasters of Jena and Auerstedt in 1806, though, these grenadier caps were done away with again.

Grenadier caps for parade use reappeared in Prussia in the 1st Foot Guard Regiment (1824), the Castle Guard Company (1829), and the Tsar Alexander Grenadier Guard Regiment No. 1 (1894).

The picture of the 18th-Century soldier was dominated by the hat or grenadier cap. It was worn by all officers, but was also the headgear of dragoons and cuirassiers. In order to offer better protection to the head, iron crosses were widely used inside hats.

After 1800 the hats became progressively higher, usually had two points and were no longer worn crosswise, but, rather, in line with the face. Rich trimmings of braid and feathers, as well as high plumes, were to increase their impressive appearance. By the beginning of the 19th Century, the hat was chiefly the headgear of generals and military officials, but it generally disappeared by the middle of the century—only in Bavaria was the general's hat retained until 1902 or, in some cases, 1912. In 1893 the German troops in Africa were again outfitted with hats, now with the left brim turned up and the imperial cockade affixed.

Typical Hussar headgear included the fez-like "wing cap" and the fur cap, both of which originated in the Turkish "kalpak" or Hungarian "kalpag", a high cylindrical cap made of cloth, felt or fur.

The wing cap was made of thick felt. A suitable "wing" was placed around the body of the cap and worn either hooked fast or hanging down. The inside of the wing was lined with colored cloth in the regimental color. Various emblems and plumes were worn in numerous ways.

The Hussars' fur cap had a more expansive shape and a pouch attached to the crown and hanging down—the color varied according to the regiment. This pouch was a carryover from the original pointed cap. Fur caps appeared with the first Hussar regiments at the beginning of the 16th Century and characterized the appearance of Hussars into the present century. The wing caps disappeared around 1800. but reappeared in the active Hussar regiments in Prussia between 1843 and 1850, and were still worn among the home guards until after 1870.

Prussia: Guard's star for officers of the Hussar Guards, as of 1860.

Since the headgear used previously did not offer the needed protection in battle, Marshal Moritz of Saxony developed the so-called "casquette" in France in the mid-18th Century. This was a helmet with a body of sheet metal or iron, covered with cloth or fur. A metal crest was attached to the round headpiece to protect against stabbing. Strands of hair hanging down were supposed to enhance the martial appearance, and plumes of feathers on the side served for identification as well as decoration. (Behavioral scientists have seen in the use of hair and feather plumes at all times a concealed symbolism indicative of an imposing, powerful air, as, for example, the horse was regarded as a magic creature with supernatural powers and the rooster was seen as a symbol of alertness and fighting spirit).

The casquette, originally very low, grew to a considerable height around 1800, and was made out of metal as well as leather. The bows or crests on the helmet were no longer made only of metal, but also of leather or leather-covered wood, and there was usually a ball of horsehair, fur or other material on the bow. Its purpose, in addition to adding impressive height, was to offer additional protection. The best-known type of casquette was the Bavarian "crested helmet" that characterized the appearance of the Bavarian soldier for almost ninety years. Although it was highly criticized from the start in many armies, this helmet was always retained despite all the suggestions made for new headgear—and many were made. In the end, when new types of headgear were again discussed in 1868, the "crest that characterizes the Bavarian helmet and awakens historical memories" was again retained at the personal wish of King Ludwig II. Only after the death of Ludwig II in 1886 was the "Pickelhaube" introduced in Bavaria.

Prussia: Helmet eagle of officers of the line Grenadier Regiment, as of 1860.

The Bavarian helmet, with its varying models, constantly reduced in size and weight, shows that efforts were made to decrease the burdensome nature of all early 19th-Century helmets. In almost all regimental histories there are complaints about the weight and rigidity of the high casquettes and helmets.

Especially impressive examples of helmets with crests are the Bavarian officer's helmet of the Gardes du Corps in 1814 and its Saxon counterpart of 1810, as well as the 1809 Prussian cuirassier's helmet, which was based on a type used in Russia since 1803.

Before the crested helmet, Bavarian soldiers had worn the so-called "Rumford hat", introduced by Count Rumford as part of a far-reaching military reorganization between 1789 and 1800. This hat, sometimes also called a casquette, was made of pressed black-lacquered leather (or felt) and bore a small brass shield with the Bavarian electoral arms on the front. The low form, the horizontal front peak and the hanging horsehair "caterpillar" made this hat quite unattractive, with the result that this impractical and unappealing helmet soon disappeared—aside from Bavaria, it turned up briefly in Württemberg (1799) and Austria (1792).

In the Napoleonic Wars a new type of fighting force appeared, coming from Poland: the Uhlans or mounted lancers ("lanciers" in French). These troops brought along a new and different type of headgear: the Uhlan's chapka. The chapka was a high helmet with a four-cornered leather crown, its sides being made of cloth stiffened with reeds. The Uhlans' weapon was quickly accepted in numerous armies, and the chapka became part of the general helmet development, steadily becoming lower and more elegantly shaped. In 1867 the neck of the chapka finally became so small and low that the emblem was attached to the crown from then on.

The dominant type of military headgear in the first half of the 19th Century was the shako. This hat had been developed in France, based on the civilian top hat that appeared in the 1780's. Other sources say that the shako was developed from the old casquette in Austria. It must be noted that the Austrian casquette, with its upright front shield and nearly cylindrical crown, was not unlike a shako, lacking only the front and rear peaks. And the term "c̀sakó" comes from Hungarian, is related to the German word "Zacken" and originally described an indented "Zackenhut", as Transfeld writes—thus the Austro-Hungarian origin of the shako is quite possible.

The shako is usually made of heavy felt, has a round leather crown, a leather band and front and rear peaks of the same material. V-shaped leather stiffeners are often sewn on the sides as well. Over the years the shako went through many changes, becoming wider and lower, higher and narrower, or having a horizontal or very raked crown (the so-called Russian "Kiwer" form). All in all, the shako remained the most lasting form of helmet, appearing in Prussia for the first time in 1801 as a test model and being retained for use by the Jäger and mobile troops until the end of World War I. After that, the shako was the typical headgear of the police for half a century.

Inevitably, the shako too was decorated with plumes or pompoms, emblems or even oversize plumes which, in Prussia, grew to half a meter in length, a fad of the 1820's.

Bavaria: Shako emblem for Jäger officers, as of 1895.

Reports from every imaginable military reporter agree in their complaint that the helmets of the early 19th Century were ill-fitting and burdensome. The crested helmets in particular, with their woven fur trim, were not only nesting places for vermin of all kinds, but became even heavier when they soaked up rain. Help first came in the form of the peaked cap, which developed from the common soldier's stable cap around 1810, originally being nothing more than a pointed cap often called the "wood cap" in the army. The stable cap was worn more and more in place of a helmet. But the peaked cap was reserved for officers (and non-commissioned officers), and enlisted men wore peakless service caps in the old army until 1918. The ranks were granted the desirable peaked cap as a regular piece of their outfits only with the formation of the Reichswehr in 1919.

Soon the officers of Napoleon's day appeared only in the peaked cap, while the uncomfortable helmet was left at home.

Headgear retained its Napoleonic size into the Thirties; then in 1842, the decisive uniform innovation took place in Prussia: the helmet with a point on top and the service jacket were introduced. The shako and the old helmet disappeared along with the uniform coat. Along with the new uniform came the new helmet, which was carelessly or satirically called the "Pickelhaube."

Mecklenburg-Schwerin: Helmet emblem as of 1866.

There are several stories concerning the existence of this new Prussian helmet. According to one anecdote, the Prussian King Friedrich Wilhelm IV saw the prototype of a pointed helmet on the desk of the Russian Tsar Nicholas I (1825-1855) during a state visit, copied the idea and put the helmet into production more quickly than the slow-moving Russians. According to other stories, the historic painter Heinrich Stilke (1803-1860) was commissioned by the King of Prussia to design such a helmet. The metallic goods manufacturer Wilhelm Jaeger of Elberstadt is also said to have supplied the design as well as the prototype of the helmet in sheet steel. The Bavarian painter Moritz von Schwind may also have been involved in the creation of the new helmet. A fresco painted by him in the Knights' Hall of Hohenschwangau Castle in 1835-36 shows, among other things, a pointed helmet very similar to the Prussian pattern of 1841, so that one could draw the conclusion that Stilke was connected with the matter. According to Transfeldt, the name originated in the word "Beckenhaube", a medieval sheet-metal helmet. During the course of time, the word, which originated from the basin-shaped form, then turned to "Beckel-, Bickel- and finally Pickelhaube." The name of the helmet itself presumably had nothing to do with the point. "Pickel" is supposed to refer only to the shape of the helmet, but not to the Orientally influenced point (compare the Persian cavalry helmets with four-sided points, which were used since the 15th Century). In any case, this linguistic development of the term "Pickelhaube" sounds a bit contrived, since this type of headgear was known officially simply as a "Helm", while the term "Pickelhaube" can be regarded simply as a satirical name. One could debate the question of whether the typical citizen would be more inclined toward the concept of "picken"—to stick or stab—or "Buckel"—a bulge ("Beulenhaube").

The newly-created Prussian uniform and helmet remained characteristic of German military dress for more than seventy years, until the middle of World War I, for slowly but surely the uniforms of all the German states followed the Prussian model; even Bavaria came under the "Pickelhaube" after the death of King Ludwig II in 1886; Prince Regent Luitpold (1886-1912) steadfastly defended the hat for the Bavarian generals, but never in his life wore a "Pickelhaube" himself, and even though he introduced the pointed helmet for generals in 1902, he required the hat with golden embroidery for the royal adjutants who surrounded him every day.

The Prussian pointed helmet was first used in a high, almost oversize form. The helmet was made out of leather as well as metal, with the metal version used only by the cuirassiers, while all other troops wore the leather type. The Hussars with their wing and fur caps were naturally an exception, as were the Uhlans with their chapka. The infantry guards, as before, wore their grenadier caps only for parades; otherwise they wore the earlier shako or the "Pickelhaube."

Over the years the "Pickelhaube" became lower, its form more pleasant, and its weight was cut down. Experiments in weight reduction (in 1867) by leaving off the front and rear peaks on the brims and crown were not successful. The metal cuirassier's helmet (made of sheet tombac for the guards and the Brandenburg Cuirassier Regiment) likewise underwent changes, of which the most noteworthy—other than its reduced height—was the smooth, no longer channeled front peak of the 1899 enlisted men's model.

Despite all the improvements and changes, the experiences of World War I showed that the leather helmet, and even the thin metal helmet worn by the cuirassiers, could no longer withstand the penetrating power of modern bullets, as the vast number of head wounds proved. In particular, in modern-day warfare it is not the soldier's optical impression that is of prime importance, but rather camouflage and protection, so that the decisive criteria of earlier days, such as colorful, glittering helmets, bright plumes and attachments, were eliminated along with impractical materials such as fur, leather or cloth. The result of these considerations was the steel helmet introduced in the German army in 1916, designed by the surgeon Dr. August Bier and Professor Friedrich Schwerd. Steel helmets were introduced in other states too, but it is undeniable that the German steel helmet was best of all, not only practically but esthetically too.

Seen in this light, headgear forms a circle, leading from the medieval iron helmet to the steel helmet. To this day, the steel helmet characterizes the appearance of the fighting soldier all over the world.

Prussia: Officer's cartridge case of the Cavalry Guard, circa 1830.

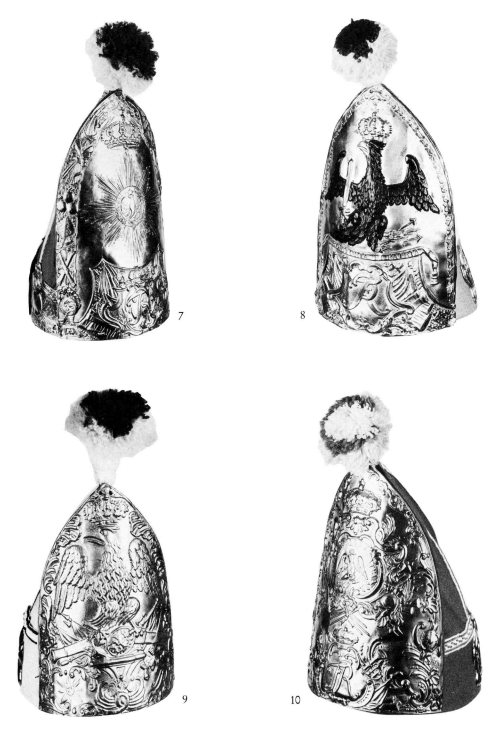

7 Prussia: Grenadier cap of the "Grenadier Guard" Infantry Regiment (Old Prussian No. 6), also called the "Giant Guards" or "King's Regiment." 1729 model, made in 1739.

8 Prussia: Grenadier cap of the "Prince of Prussia" Infantry Regiment (Old Prussian No. 18), 1744.

9 Prussia: Grenadier cap of Garrison Grenadier V, as of 1741.

10 Prussia: Grenadier cap of the "Markgraf Heinrich" Infantry Regiment (Old Prussian No. 42), 1741.

11-13 Prussia: Bombardier caps, worn from 1731 to 1786. Black oilcloth with brass trim.

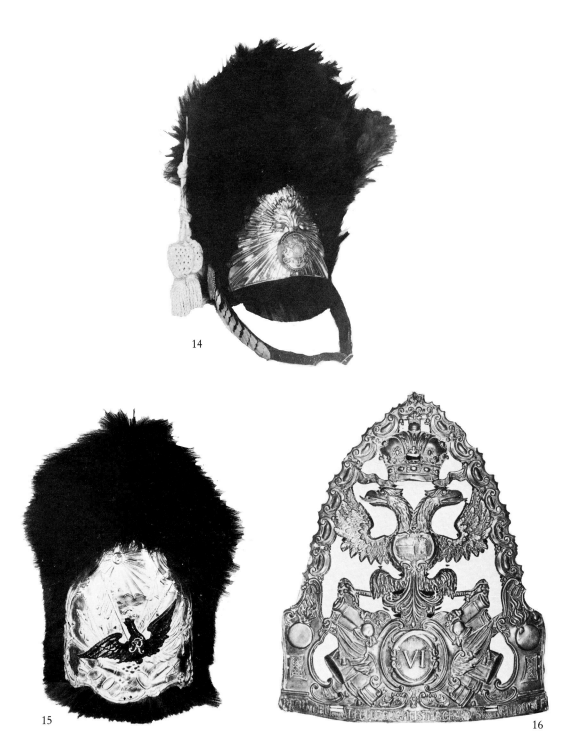

14

15

16

14 Hannover: Bearskin cap for enlisted men of the Grenadier Guard Battalion, 1833-1838. With gilded shield and chains, white pendants, and red plume at the left for musicians.

15 Prussia: Bearskin grenadier cap of a free battalion, after 1757. (After the battle of Rossbach, November 5, 1757, the heraldic sun emblem was shown.)

16 First German Empire: Grenadier cap brass of the regiment of Ordnance Master General Count von Seckendorff, 1723-1742.

17 Prussia:Grenadier cap for enlisted men of the 1st Battalion of the 1st Foot Guard Regiment; M/1824. The "Semper Talis" bandeau was granted in 1889. In 1894 the 1st Guard Regiment gave these caps to the Tsar Alexander Grenadier Guard Regiment No. 1, and the bandeau was removed; thus these caps were worn with holes in the shield until they were replaced.

18 Prussia: Grenadier cap of the 1st and 2nd Battalions of the 1st Foot Guard Regiment, M/1894. Originally worn without a chain, which was introduced only in 1896. (Here the chains were taken off the helmets so the helmets would stand upright without them. This explains why the chains are often missing from grenadier caps.) Red cloth with white woolen braid.

19 Prussia: Grenadier officer's cap of the 1st and 2nd Battalions, 1st Guard Regiment, M/1894. The field mark of silver fringe was called a "plum." The cloth, unlike that of the enlisted men, is set off with silver braid.

20 Prussia: Grenadier cap of the 3rd Battalion, 1st Guard Regiment, M/1894. Here the bandeau reads "Pro Gloria et Patria" and the cloth is yellow.

21 Prussia: Grenadier officer's cap of the Tsar Alexander Guard Regiment No. 1, M/1894, with enameled guard star.

22 Prussia: Fusilier cap (enlisted man) of the 3rd Battalion of the Tsar Alexander Grenadier Guard Regiment. The caps of the 3rd Battalion were lower, the shape not concave but running straight up to the point. The chains were not held by clasps but by screws, with an eagle over and to the rear of each.

23 Prussia: Grenadier cap for enlisted men of the 1st and 2nd Battalions of the Tsar Alexander Grenadier Guard Regiment. New type made after 1900, without holes.

26 Prussia: Hat for enlisted naval men, 1848.

27 Prussia: Officer's hat of the Royal Prussian Infantry Regiment of Fouqué (Old Prussian No. 33), circa 1745.

28 Prussia: "Casquette" or two-lapped musketeer hat, this one from the Infantry Regiment of Kleist (Old Prussian No. 12), 1787-1798.

29 Bavaria: General's hat, M/1873, with white and blue rooster feathers, worn until 1902. The trim was gold for generals' adjutants.

30 Prussia: Officer's hat of the Royal Prussian Infantry Regiment von Puttkamer (Old Prussian No. 36), 1803-1806.

31 Prussia: Peaked cap for infantry officers, the last and most elegant type, circa 1914.

32 Prussia: Oilcloth Home Guard cap, 1914-1918. Model with certificate, which served as a test piece for manufacturing.

33 Braunschweig: Peaked cap for officers of Hussar Regiment No. 17, with the special death's-head emblem, circa 1914.

34 Bavaria: Peaked cap of the motorized corps, made of leather (for better protection in bad weather), circa 1915.

35 Imperial Germany: Cap for seamen of the Imperial Navy, here the naval artillery, circa 1912.

36 Imperial Germany: Hat (two-pointed) for officers of the Imperial Navy, circa 1910.

37 German Empire: Hat for officers of the German protective troops in Southwest Africa, with light blue hatband (this was white for East Africa, red for Cameroon and Togo), circa 1914.

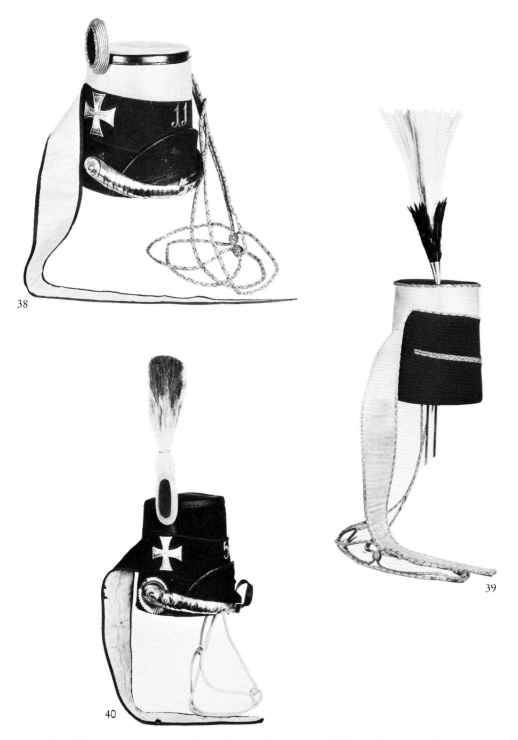

38 Prussia: Officer's wing cap M/1843, of the 11th Home Guard Hussar Regiment (belonging to the 3rd Westphalian Home Guard Regiment No. 16).

39 Prussia: Officer's wing cap, M/1843, from the 1st Silesian Hussar Regiment No. 4, with hawk's-feather parade plume.

40 Prussia: Wing cap for enlisted men of the 5th Home Guard Hussar Regiment (belonging to the 4th Pomeranian Home Guard Regiment No. 21), worn as of 1852.

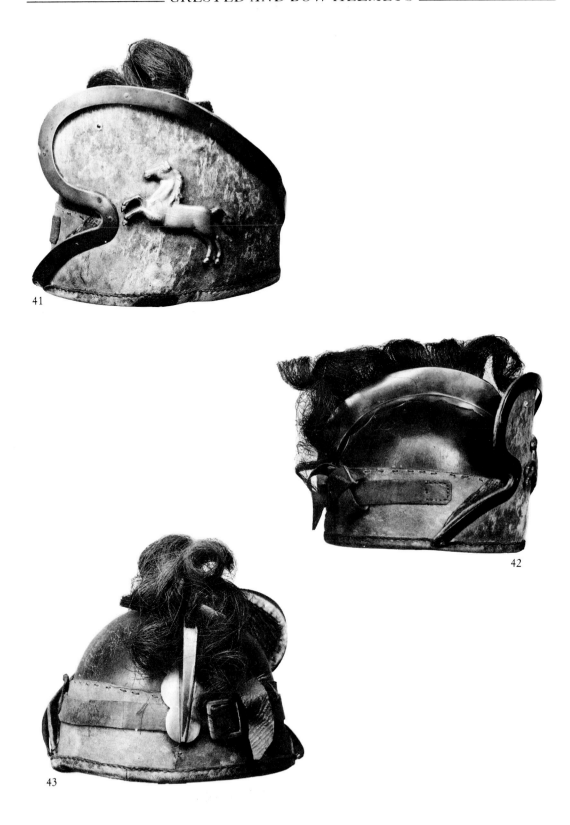

41-43 Hannover: Helmets for enlisted men of the 9th Light Dragoon Regiment, 1763-1803. Leather; shield with fur trim, iron mounting.

46 Prussia: Helmet for enlisted men of the line cuirassier regiments, M/1808 (high crown, low crest). Brass shield with raised eagle.

47 Oldenburg: Dragoon enlisted men's helmet, probably not the official model introduced under Duke Paul Friedrich August, circa 1840-1842.

48 Prussia: Helmet for enlisted men of the guard cuirassiers, in post-1830 form (low crown, high crest). Brass shield with attached silver guard star (for the Garde du Corps, the star was stamped into the shield).

49 Baden: Enlisted men's helmet of the 2nd Dragoon Regiment of Geusau, established 1813, worn until 1818.

50 Bavaria: Enlisted men's helmet of the Garde du Corps, 1814, of sheet brass, with the monogram of King Max I Joseph (1806-1825).

51 Bavaria: Enlisted men's helmet of the Prince Karl of Bavaria Cuirassier Regiment, M/1814, helmet made of sheet iron.

52 Bavaria: Enlisted men's helmet of the Garde du Corps, 1814, side view.

53 Bavaria: Cuirassier officer's helmet M/1833, with monogram of King Ludwig I (1825-1848). Form somewhat lower, chains no longer attached to Medusa heads but to lions' heads.

54 Bavaria: Cuirassier officer's helmet, M/1843. After the suggested Prussian model was rejected, a lighter cuirassier helmet was introduced for the ranks in 1842 (retained until 1879). For the officers, a helmet was introduced as M/1843 which still had the leather straps with silvered oak leaves. Only a few of these helmets could have been made, as the old helmets were still worn; on the other hand, a new officer's helmet, made completely of sheet German silver and without straps or oak leaves, was introduced in 1845.

57 Bavaria: Casquette for enlisted men of the 1st Jäger Battalion, M/1815, garrisoned in Salzburg 1815-1819, then in Burghausen, with woven fur crest.

58 Bavaria: Casquette for light cavalry officers, M/1832, with bearskin crest.

59 Bavaria: Jäger helmet, M/1845, with one-piece yellow trim.

70 Bavaria: Infantry officer's helmet, M/1861, with "sun emblem" with monogram of King Maximilian II (1848-1864).

71 Bavaria: Helmet for a non-commissioned officer of the reserve home guard, M/1873, "sun emblem" with monogram of King Ludwig II (1864-1886). The helmet bowl of the 1868 model was made lower again in 1873.

72 Bavaria: Helmet for infantry officers, M/1868. The "L" and crown emblem was now made in two pieces.

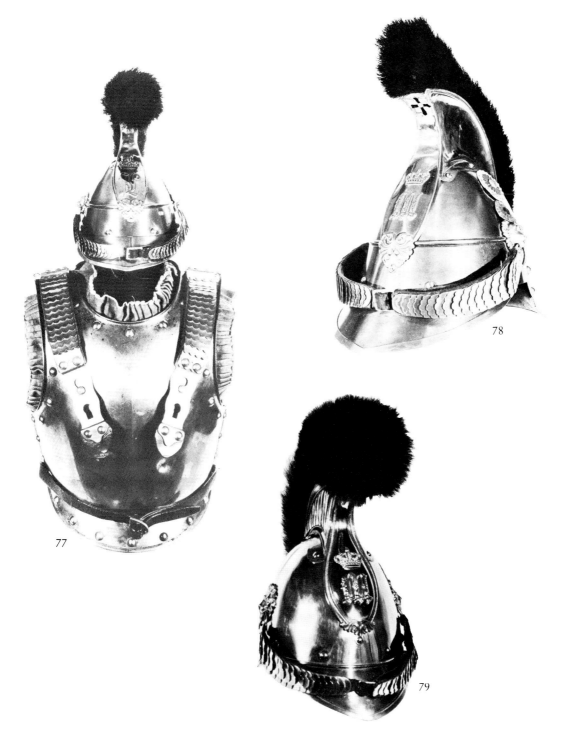

77 Bavaria: Helmet M/1842 for cuirassier enlisted men, plus cast steel cuirass M/1845, test model.

78 Bavaria: Enlisted men's helmet M/1842 for cuirassiers, with monogram of King Maximilian II as of 1848 and federation cockade worn by the Bavarians from 1848 to 1851.

79 Bavaria: Cuirassier officer's helmet M/1845, with monogram of King Maximilian II, made of sheet German silver, partly gilded.

80 Bavaria: Cuirassier officer's helmet M/1873, flat form, of sheet iron, worn until 1879, the cuirass itself having been eliminated in 1873.

81 Braunschweig: Artillery officer's helmet, introduced in 1839 superseding the Bavarian M/1832. Gilded trim, bearskin crest. Worn until 1866, then replaced by the shako.

82 Hannover: Helmet for Garde du Corps officers, M/1840, leather with gilded shield and partly silvered trim. Replaced in 1849 by a Prussian model metal helmet.

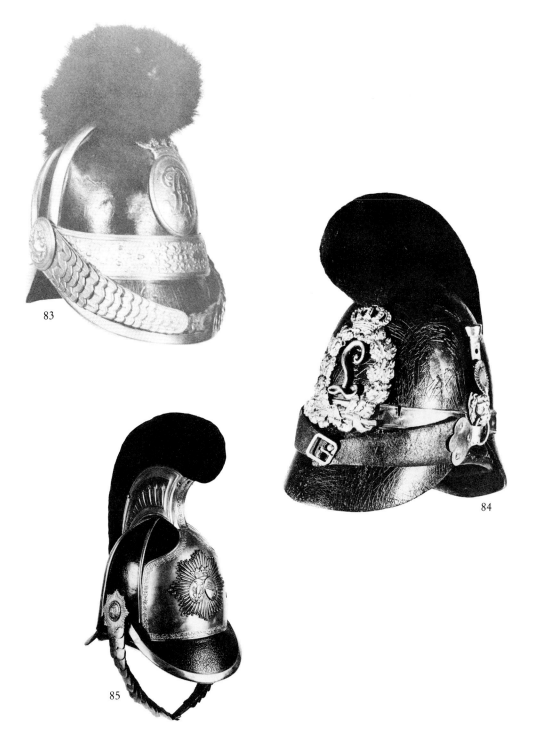

83 Saxony: Officer's helmet of the mounted artillery units, M/1843, worn until 1867. Likewise identical to the Bavarian M/1832 type, with monogram of King Johann (as of 1854).

84 Baden: Artillery enlisted men's helmet, based on the Bavarian model, worn from 1834 to 1849, with the monogram of Grand Duke Leopold I (1830-1852).

85 Hansa Cities: Enlisted men's helmet M/1834, of the Hanseatic cavalry division, version used by the joint Bremen-Lübeck squadron. Worn until 1850, with silvered, partly gilded trim.

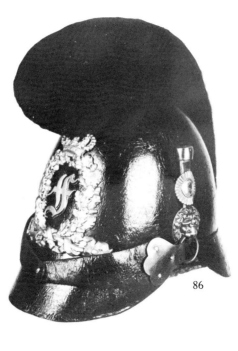

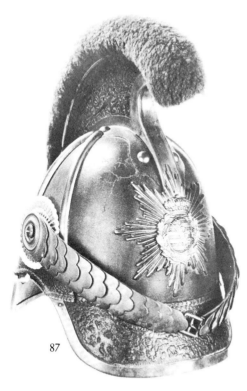

86 Baden: Enlisted men's helmet for the artillery under Grand Duke Friedrich I (regent 1852-1856), worn until about 1854.

87 Saxony: Enlisted men's helmet of the cavalry regiments, M/1867, worn until 1890, then replaced by a Prussian design.

88 Saxony: Officer's helmet of the cavalry regiments, M/1867.

89 Prussia: Officer's shako of the 2nd Brandenburg Hussar Regiment. M/1808.

90 Prussia: Shako for enlisted men of Fusilier Regiments 1 to 12, 1813.

91 Prussia: Home guard shako for enlisted men, 1813-1815, in the firm of the Russian Kiwer shako; black oilcloth on cardboard.

92 Prussia: Enlisted men's shako for infantry regiments (fusilier shako), with red horsehair plume for parade use by musicians, 1813 model.

93 Prussian: Officer's shako of Line Jäger Battalions 1, 2, 5 and 6, 1854 model.

94 Prussian: Enlisted men's shako for the Line Jäger Battalions 2, 4, 7 and 8, 1854 parade model.

95 Prussia: Enlisted men's shako for the Westphalian Jäger Battalion No. 7 of Cleve. With chinstrap hooks, M/1887. Since this means of attachment, also prescribed for helmets, did not work well, it was replaced in 1891 by the M/91 buttons used to the end.

96 Prussia: Shako M/1890 for officers of the Hannover Jäger Battalion No. 10, with the bandeau of honor granted in 1899.

97 Prussia: Shako for enlisted men of Jäger units, made of substitute material (green oilcloth), spring 1915.

98 Imperial Germany: Shako for reserve officers of sea battalions (Naval Infantry), M/1883.

99 Hannover: Shako of a cannoneer of the artillery foot batteries, circa 1820; yellow trim, strap missing.

100 Hannover: Shako M/1860 of a subaltern officer of the line infantry. On the emblem is the monogram of King Georg V (1851-1866). These shakos were patterned after an Austrian model.

101 Hannover: Shako of a sergeant of the Guard Regiment, M/1860.

102 Braunschweig: Shako for enlisted men of the 2nd (Braunschweig) Battery of Field Artillery Regiment 46, as worn from 1868 to 1886.

103 Braunschweig: Shako for enlisted men of the 1st and 2nd Battalions of Infantry Regiment 92, as worn from 1867 to 1886.

104 Braunschweig: Shako for reserve officers of the 1st and 2nd Battalions, Infantry Regiment 92, 1867-1886.

106 Saxony-Anhalt: Shako for Infantry Officers, circa 1830, with white and green horsehair plume.

107 Saxony: Shako for enlisted men of infantry brigades, with emblem of a 12th company. Introduced in 1846, worn in this form under King Johann (1854-1873) until replaced by the Pickelhaube in 1867.

108 Saxony: Officer's shako from the 1st Jäger Battalion No. 12 of Freiberg, as worn until 1897 (with Imperial cockade).

109 Saxony: Maneuver shako of oilcloth for Jäger officers, circa 1890.

110 Saxony: Shako for non-commissioned infantry officers, M/1832, worn until 1846, with white and green feather plume.

111 Württemberg: Shako for enlisted men of Training Battalion 13, 1892. (Prussian M/1860).

112 Baden: Shako for enlisted men of Training Battalion 14, 1860-1891.

113 Bavaria: Shako for officers of the airship and aviator battalions, 1911-1918. This version worn as of 1915, with chains on rosettes over 91 buttons (worn in the field with a chinstrap).

114 Bavaria: Wartime substitute for a Jäger shako, made of one piece of pressed felt, worn in 1915.

115 Mecklenburg-Schwerin: Shako for officers of Jäger Battalion No. 14 of Colmar, Alsace, as worn from 1897 on.

116 Bavaria: Shako for police officers, M/1848. With city coat of arms (Wasserburg on the Inn). Black oilcloth on cardboard.

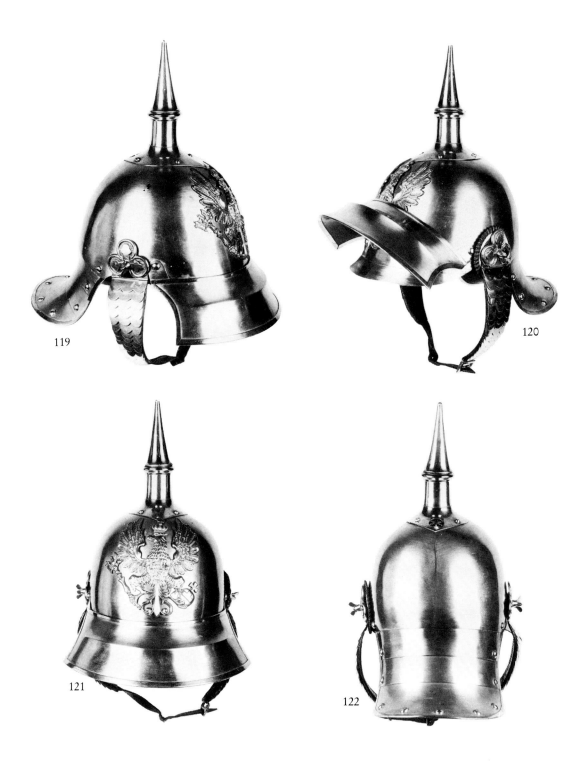

119-122 The only surviving original of the test helmet for Prussian cuirassiers, made in 1841 by the firm of Wilhelm Jaeger in Elberfeld, and probably designed there too. This test helmet was offered to all (interested) German states, including Bavaria, which declined it. With small modifications, this helmet was introduced in 1842-1843 for the Prussian cuirassiers. The folding front visor in particular, which was supposed to afford better sight in dim light or simply make wearing the helmet more convenient "out of battle", was not accepted. The pictures show the helmet from all sides.

123 Prussia: Cuirassier officer's helmet M/1843. For Line Regiments 1 to 5, 7 and 8 the helmets were made of sheet iron with gilded decorations, while the two guard regiments and the 6th Cuirassier Regiment wore helmets of tombac with German silver trim.

124 Prussia: Helmet for officers of the heavy cavalry regiments (home guard cavalry), with home guard cross on the eagle. Clear to see in the M/1843 is the externally riveted front visor, which was riveted inside as of 1853 so that no water ran into the soldier's face between the helmet and visor when it rained. The cockade of this helmet was made of silk; there were also cockades of pressed leather and sheet metal.

125 Prussia: Officer's helmet, M/1843, of the Brandenburg Cuirassier Regiment (Tsar Nicholas I of Russia) No. 6. Despite the black-and-white photo, the gleaming gold tombac can be recognized.

126 Prussia: Enlisted men's helmet for line cuirassiers, M/1853/60, of iron with brass trim. The visor is now riveted from inside, the chains are fastened to screws, since the earlier projective screws were not practical (as of 1862). The eagle bears the bandeau of the Fatherland, introduced in 1860, which is not yet stamped in but soldered onto the earlier eagle.

128 Prussia: Officer's helmet, M/1843, of the Queen's Cuirassier Regiment (Pomeranian) No. 2, Pasewalk. With the bandeau granted in 1845 in remembrance of the battle of Hohenfriedberg on June 4, 1745; this was stamped onto the eagle as of 1861.

129 Prussia: Officer's helmet of the Great Elector Cuirassier Life Guard Regiment (Silesian) No. 1, Breslau, M/1902. The officers of this regiment wore flat chains with edge piping.

130 Prussia: Enlisted men's helmet M/1889/94, from the Queen's Cuirassier Regiment.

131 Prussia: Officer's helmet, M/1889, of the Queen's Cuirassier Regiment.

132 Electoral Hesse: Officer's helmet of the Garde du Corps Regiment, M/1846. Tombac with enameled star of the Order of the Golden Lion. Worn until the regiment was disbanded in 1866.

133 Oldenburg: Dragoon officer's helmet, M/1849, worn until 1864, then replaced by caps. Sheet German silver with gilded trim.

134 Mecklenburg-Schwerin: Dragoon officer's helmet, M/1847, worn until 1865. German silver with gilded trim.

135 Hamburg: Dragoon officer's helmet, M/1850, German silver with gilded trim, worn until 1866.

137 Schleswig-Holstein: Dragoon officer's helmet, M/1848, worn until 1850. Sheet iron with gilded trim.

138 Prussia: Officer's helmet, M/1867, of the Queen's Cuirassier Regiment, in the "stylish" flat form of the 1880's.

139 Hannover: Enlisted men's helmet, M/1849, of the cuirassier guards, with white parade plume; iron with brass trim.

140 Prussia: Helmet M/1889 for life guard gendarmes, nickel-plated iron with yellow trim and German silver guard star, and gilded parade eagle.

141 Prussia: Helmet for officers of the Gardes du Corps and Cuirassier Guard Regiments, M/1889, post-1897 version, with silvered parade eagle.

142 Prussia: Helmet for enlisted men of the Cuirassier Guards, M/1843, parade version.

143 Prussia: Helmet for enlisted men of the Cuirassier Guards, M/1889/94, with parade eagle.

144 Prussia: Helmet for trumpeters of the Cuirassier Guards, parade version, M/1867. From 1843 to 1890 the trumpeters wore a red horsehair plume with German silver funnel on parade; only afterward was the eagle added.

145 Saxony: Helmet M/1890 for cavalry guards, with the lion about to spring, awarded in 1907, screwed on.

146 Saxony: Helmet for officers of the cavalry guards, parade version.

147 Saxony: Helmet M/1890 for enlisted men of the carbineers, with white horsehair parade plume.

148 Saxony: Helmet for carbineer reserve officers, with home guard cross under the coat of arms, parade version.

149 Prussia: Officer's helmet of the mounted Jäger regiments 1 to 7, nickeled helmet, silvered trim, gilded chains, worn thus as of 1905.

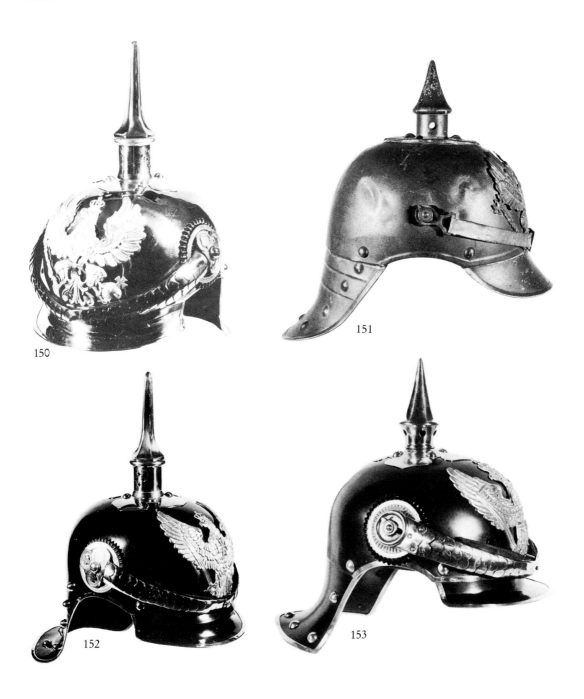

150 Prussia: Reserve officer's helmet of the line cuirassier regiments, M/1889; gilded nickel-plated trim.

151 Prussia: Wartime substitute for an enlisted men's cuirassier helmet, lacquered field gray, rivets pressed flat, with chinstrap.

152 Prussia: Officer's helmet of the mounted Jäger regiments No. 8 to 13, M/1913. Blackened sheet metal with gilded trim.

153 Prussia: Mounted Jäger enlisted men's helmet, M/1905. Blackened steel, German silver trim (for Regiments 1 to 6) and yellow chains, all trim yellow in Regiment 7. The enlisted men of Regiments 8 to 13 wore leather dragoon helmets.

162 Prussia: Officer's helmet of the Artillery Guard Brigade, M/1844. The form of the ball, originally oblong, became round toward the end of the Forties.

163 Prussia: Enlisted men's helmet of the Tsar Alexander Grenadier Guard Regiment No. 1, M/1857. Yellow trim.

164 Prussia: Officer's helmet, M/1842, of the line infantry. Gilded trim, silk cockade.

165

166

165 Prussia: Officer's helmet of the 9th Infantry Regiment (Colberg), M/1857. With bandeau of honor granted in 1849. As of 1860 the bandeau was mounted on the helmet eagle; at that time the first twelve (oldest) infantry regiments became line grenadier regiments. Gilded trim, black hair plume for parades.

166 Baden: Officer's helmet for infantry (and dragoons), M/1850. Gilded trim. When the Pickelhaube was introduced in 1849, a ball was originally worn in place of the spike; it was replaced in 1850.

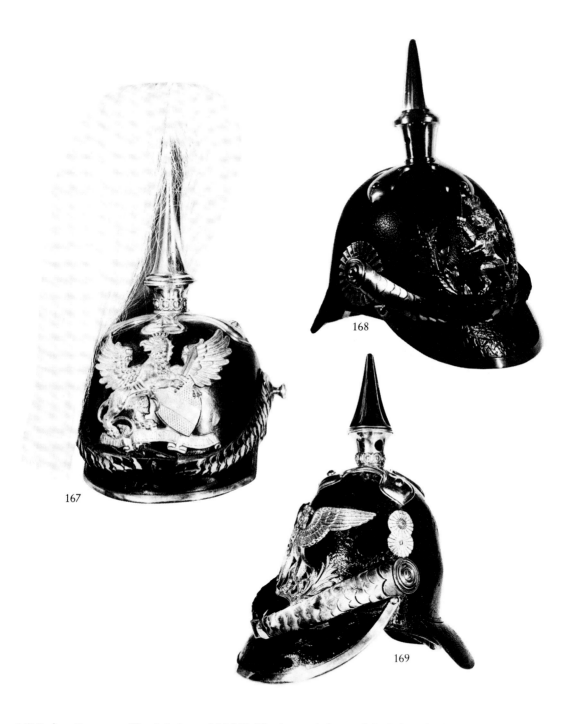

167 Baden: Dragoon officer's helmet, M/1860. The lowered shape of the helmet is clear to see. Chains still attached by screws, officer's plume still of white horsehair. White or silvered trim (matching the uniform buttons) as of 1860.

168 Hesse-Darmstadt: Officer's helmet (for all service arms), M/1849, post-1857 version, with the helmet already lowered.

169 Baden: Artillery officer's helmet, 1850-1851. With round front visor and state cockade, with the black-red-gold union cockade, introduced in Germany 1848-1851, over it.

170 Hannover: Officer's helmet, M/1849, of the line infantry. Worn until 1858 or 1860. Yellow trim with white horse figure.

171 Nassau: Infantry officer's helmet, M/1849, worn until 1862. As in Baden, at first a ball point was worn, then a four-sided spike. Gilded trim.

172 Hannover: Dragoon enlisted men's helmet, M/1849. Made of black lacquered sheet metal, with yellow trim. Worn until 1866, with a black hair plume for parades.

173 Prussia: Officer's helmet, M/1843, for gendarmes (police); gilded trim.

174 Prussia: Infantry officer's helmet, M/1860, with gilded trim. The infantry officers still had a cross, angular visor and arched chains (changed with M/1867).

175 Prussia: Infantry officer's helmet, M/1867. Now with plate base, round front visor and flat chains. The rear bar was removed but replaced in 1871, as the helmet lacked stability without it.

176 Prussia: Enlisted men's helmet, M/1887, here with the eagle of the non-commissioned officer's training schools. It was first ordered that the chains were to be worn only for parades, with a chinstrap for service. In order to make the change easy, the hook fasteners were introduced, but were not practical. The hook was replaced in 1891 with the M/91 button, which was used to the end.

177 Prussia: Infantry officer's helmet, M/1871, in form and as worn from 1897 on.

178 Braunschweig: Enlisted men's helmet of Infantry Regiment 92, worn with a death's-head until 1912 only by the 3rd Battalion, afterward prescribed for the whole regiment. On the neck of the spike is the ridge introduced in 1887 to replace the pearl ring.

179 Prussia: Enlisted men's helmet in post-1897 form, with chinstrap on M/91 buttons and pearl ring on the spike, which was officially changed to a ridge for enlisted men in 1887. Such nonstandard details were common in uniform pieces owned by the men.

154

155

156

157

154 Prussia: Officer's helmet of the 1st Foot Guard Regiment, Berlin, M/1843.

155 Baden: Infantry officer's helmet, 1849-1850. Worn with a ball instead of a spike in its first year of use.

156 Hannover: General's helmet, M/1848. The middle of the star is made of fine porcelain painting.

157 Mecklenburg-Schwerin: Enlisted men's helmet, M/1848, for infantry, worn until 1866.

208

208 Saxe-Coburg: Helmet of Duke Carl Eduard, worn as Chief of the 6th Thuringian Infantry
Regiment No. 95, with parade plume, plus the Duke's Damascus saber.

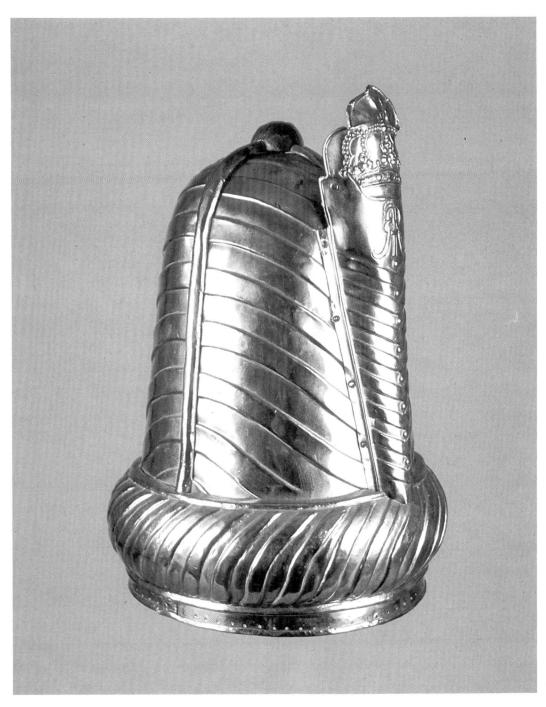

117

117 Saxony-Poland: Helmet for non-commissioned officers of the Janissary Corps, 1715-1733. Founded by Elector Friedrich August I, also King August II of Poland, popularly called "August the Strong" (born 1670, reigned 1694-1733). The Janissary officers wore richly ornamented cloth turbans, while the enlisted men wore caps. Only the non-commissioned officers had these unique gilded brass helmets, made to resemble turbans. The monogram "AR" stands for "Augustus Rex"; a feather about a meter long was worn in the socket.

118

118 Prussia: Model helmet for cuirassiers, M/1841. The "original Pickelhaube."

127

127 Prussia: Helmet for officers of the Gardes du Corps Regiment (or Cuirassier guards), M/1842, with parade eagle. On the front of the helmet is engraved the name of the former wearer. It was the custom to give the helmet to the officers' casino as a memento when one ended one's service and have one's name engraved on it.

136

136 Prussia: Enlisted men's helmet of the Gardes du Corps Regiment, M/1843, with parade eagle, plus the black cuirass, a gift of the Tsar in 1814, worn only in the spring parade.

105

105 Nassau: Subaltern officer's shako of the infantry, M/1863 (based on an Austrian model), worn until 1866.

220

220 Hamburg: Chapka for dragoon officers, 1815-1835. At first the Hamburg cavalry was organized as Uhlan squadrons (1813); as of 1834 these were changed to dragoon regiments, but the chapkas were worn until the end of the Forties.

221

221 Prussia: Chapka for enlisted men of the 2nd Uhlan Guard Regiment, Berlin, M/1843, worn in this form until 1851, the parade version is seen here.

222

222 Prussia: Chapka for officers of the Rhenish Uhlan Regiment No. 7, of Saarbrücken, M/1843 (with the 1844 eagle), parade version.

236

237

235 Bavaria: Uhlan officer's chapka, M/1864, the top still covered with cloth. The plume was not for parade but for service.

236 Bavaria: Uhlan officer's chapka, M/1873, the top now covered with black leather (to protect against wetness), the plume now the parade type, with a service emblem.

237 Bavaria: Parade uniform of a first lieutenant and adjutant of the 1st Uhlan Regiment, Kaiser Wilhelm, King of Prussia, in Bamberg, circa 1913.

238

238 Bavaria: Chapka of an officer in the 1st Uhlan Regiment, Kaiser Wilhelm, King of Prussia, in Bamberg, in parade form with facings, buffalo-hair plume, field emblem and silver-blue restraining cord, circa 1914.

260

259

262

261

Bavarian Uniforms

259 Doublet for privates of the 1st Light Cavalry Regiment, Crown Prince, Nürnberg-Bayreuth, 1835-1849.

260 Service jacket of a lieutenant in the 3rd Infantry Regiment, Prince Carl, Augsburg, 1860-1873.

261 Service jacket of a corporal in the 2nd Infantry Regiment, Crown Prince, Munich, 1860-1873.

262 Service jacket and hat (for parade) of a captain and flank adjutant of the royal adjutancy, 1873-1886.

374

374 Bavaria: Group of original uniform pieces of the home guard, from the reign of King Maximilian II. With the introduction of the service jacket in the army, the home guard also received this new uniform; at the same time, on September 28, 1848 the first ''Pickelhaube'' (center) for the home guard was introduced, and the cavalry received a bow helmet of leather modeled after the cuirassier helmet. At left is a service jacket for the cavalry, with bandolier and belted saber, at right a service jacket for fusiliers with M/1830 side arms on a buckled belt. In the foreground is a caparison for enlisted men of the cavalry, plus parts of the harness and the belt of the King's Loyal Home Guard, worn only in 1848.

387 388

389 390

Prussian Ring Collars

387 Officer of the Gardes du Corps Regiment, post-1912, for the 200th birthday of Frederick the Great.

388 Officer of the Great Elector Life Guard Cuirassier Regiment (Silesian) No. 1, Breslau, as of 1896.

389 Officer of the Queen's Cuirassier Regiment (Pomeranian) No. 2, Pasewalk, post-1895, for the 150th anniversary of the battle of Hohenfriedberg.

390 Officer of the Staff Guard at command posts, post-1893.

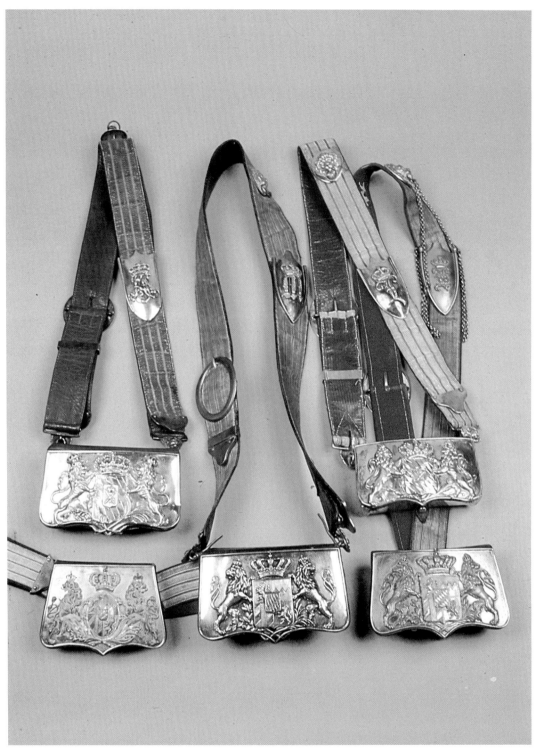

391

391 Bavaria: Collection of all the cartridge case models for the cavalry; upper row left: From the reign of Max I Joseph (1806-1825); upper right: reign of Ludwig I (1825-1848); lower left: Prince Regent Luitpold (1886-1918); center: Maximilian II (1848-1864); right: Ludwig II (1864-1886).

184 Prussia: Enlisted men's helmet for infantry guards, parade form as of 1897. The smooth shaft for the enlisted men's plume, narrowing to a pointed neck, is clear to see; the officer's funnel type spread to the width of the normal spike at the bottom.

185 Prussia: Officer's helmet of the infantry guards, post-1897 form. The color of the trim matched that of the buttons.

186 Prussia: Helmet owned by an ensign of a line dragoon regiment, in post-1897 form. After passing the officers' examination, the wearer had only to attach the star screws and the officer's cockade to have a correct officer's helmet.

187 Prussia: Field gray enlisted men's dragoon helmet, official test type of 1915.

188 Prussia: Officer's helmet of the Baron von Derfflinger (Neumarkish) Mounted Grenadier Regiment No. 3, Bromberg. This regiment was honored with the grenadier's eagle in 1897, as well as the ornamental rosettes on the chains. Silvered trim.

189 Prussia: Foot artillery officer's helmet, post-1897. The oversize neck and the extended socket of the ball, a throwback to "making an impression", are easy to see. Gilded trim.

190

191

192

190 Bavaria: Infantry reserve officer's helmet, M/1886, still with the large coat of arms. At first (until 1897) the Bavarian cockade was on the right side of the helmet and had a wavy rather than a zigzag edge.

191 Bavaria: Infantry officer's helmet with emblem, M/1896. But helmets with the big coats of arms were still worn then. The laurel and oak twig often present (and obligatory in large coats of arms) cannot be traced to any particular troop unit either from documents or photographs.

192 Bavaria: Officer's helmet of the 1st Heavy Cavalry Regiment of Prince Karl of Bavaria, Munich. Parade type worn since 1897.

193 Bavaria: Enlisted men's helmet, M/1897, for heavy cavalry. The first "Pickelhaube" in the Bavarian Army, introduced during the reign of King Ludwig II. Practically a crested helmet M/1873 with a spike added instead of the crest.

194 Bavaria: Enlisted men's helmet, M/1886, for infantry. Yellow trim, chains already attached by M/91 buttons. At first the infantry helmet also had arched chains (as of 1913, "slightly arched" chains were introduced again.

195 Bavaria: Enlisted men's helmet for the infantry, M/1896. Now following the Prussian pattern with an attached plate. The coat of arms is likewise smaller and made of "aluminum bronze"; like the "L" initials of the crested helmets, it could not be cleaned, as it bore a protective lacquer.

196

197

198

196 Bavaria: Officer's helmet of the foot artillery, M/1915. At first the Bavarian artillery was to wear the ball point (on a cross mount), but this rarely took place, as very few officers followed the new prescription (which was also intended for "future peacetime").

197 Bavaria: Infantry helmet in wartime substitute form, made of field gray painted sheet metal, all in one piece. A further variation of the many test helmets made in Bavaria by, among others, the sheet-metal toy manufacturers, the Bing Brothers, in Nürnberg.

198 Baden: Infantry officer's helmet, post-1897 form, with gilded trim.

199 Hesse-Darmstadt: officer's helmet of the Life Guard Infantry Regiment (1st Grand Ducal Hessian) No. 115, of Darmstadt. Post-1897 form, with parade plume. Varied from the usual Hessian helmets with star screws and flat chains (the Grand Duke himself wore this type of helmet).

200 Baden: Field artillery officer's helmet, post-1897 form, with gilded trim.

201 Hesse-Darmstadt: Infantry officer's helmet, post-1897. Hessian officers, atypically, wore no star screws on the (smooth) cross mount, but always wore arched chains, even the foot troops. (For an exception, see #199.)

202 Mecklenburg-Strelitz: officer's helmet of the 2nd Battalion of Grenadier Regiment No. 89, of Neustrelitz. Post-1897 form, with gilded trim.

203 Oldenburg: Helmet owned by a sergeant of Dragoon Regiment No. 19. Silvered trim, post-1897 form.

204 Mecklenburg-Schwerin: Enlisted men's helmet of the 1st and 3rd Battalions of Grenadier Regiment No. 89, in 1867-1890 form.

205

206

207

205 Saxony: Infantry enlisted men's helmet, M/1867, with yellow trim.

206 Mecklenburg-Schwerin: Reserve officer's helmet of Dragoon Regiment No. 17, of Ludwigslust, post-1897 form.

207 Saxony: Helmet for generals, post-1897 form, with colorful enamel star and gilded trim.

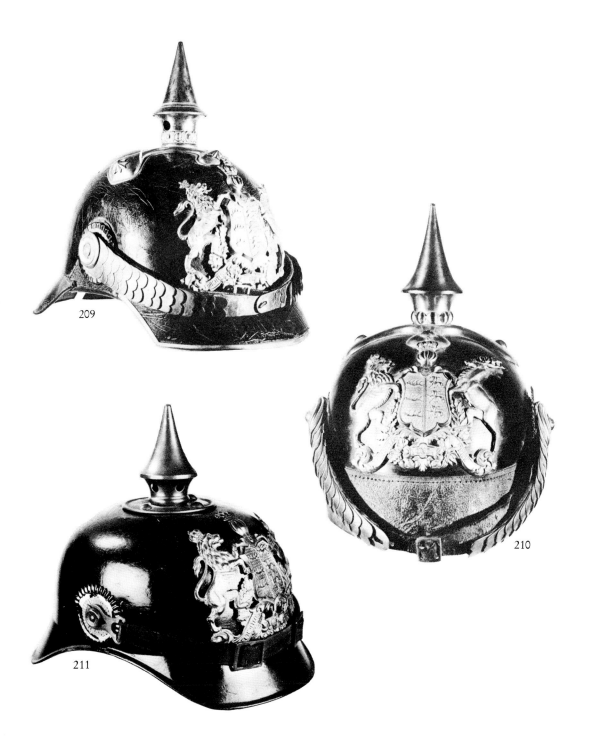

209 Württemberg: Infantry officer's helmet, M/1871, with the state cockade still worn to the right; gilded trim.

210 Württemberg: Infantry enlisted men's helmet, M/1871, with yellow trim, circa 1895.

211 Württemberg: Infantry enlisted men's helmet, 1915 substitute product made of black lacquered sheet metal, with yellow trim.

212 Württemberg: Engineer officer's helmet, post-1897 form, with silvered trim.

213 Württemberg: Artillery enlisted men's helmet with field gray trim, 1915.

214 Württemberg: Infantry enlisted men's helmet, substitute product of cork with cloth cover, yellow trim, simplified chinstrap, worn in the summer of 1815.

215

216

215 Bavaria: Officer's chapka, M/1813, of the (1st) Uhlan Regiment, worn until the regiment was disbanded in 1822. The hanging plume was worn from 1817 on; previously a standing white horsehair plume was used. Yellow cloth on Spanish reed, "industriously sewn."

216 Prussia: Chapka for officers of the home guard cavalry, M/1808, this version circa 1820. Blue cloth cover, particularly long restraining cord that was worn wrapped several times around the body.

217 Prussia: Service chapka for Uhlan officers, of black leather, without an eagle, with faint leather emblem. Non-regulation but often-worn substitute for the usually prescribed chapka with a black oilcloth cover. Worn until 1867.

218 Prussia: Officer's chapka, M/1862, from Uhlan Regiment 4 or 8. The eagle, still worn on the neck, is missing.

219 Prussia: Officer's chapka, M/1862, from the 1st Brandenburg Uhlan Regiment (Tsar of Russia) No. 3 (transferred to Saxony). It follows the 1862 model, but is similar to the higher form of the 1843 model, but with a front bar. The officers of this regiment received in 1862, as a special honor, a broad gold braid of Russian pattern, which was hooked around the crown. Yellow cloth cover.

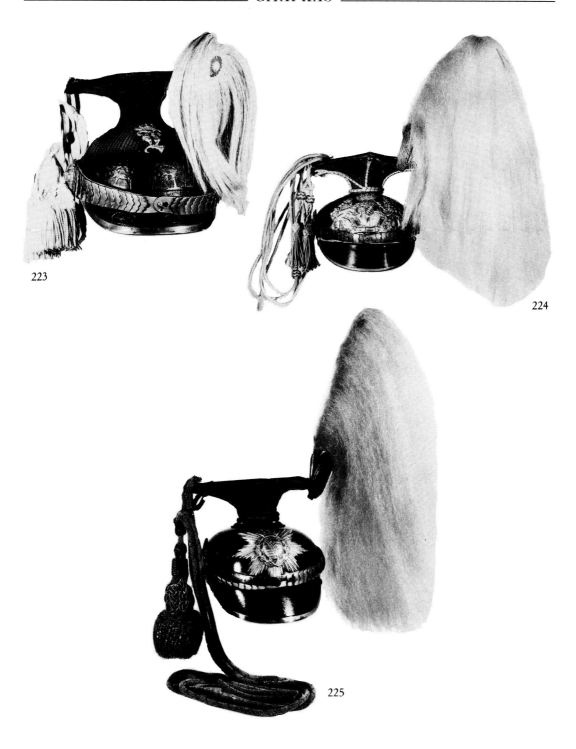

223 Bavaria: Chapka M/1873 for enlisted men of the two Uhlan regiments, with parade plume and red cloth cover.

224 Bavaria: Chapka M/1886 for an ensign of the 1st Kaiser Wilhelm, King of Prussia Uhlan Regiment, of Bamberg; in parade form.

225 Saxony: Officer's chapka M/1867, this version for the 3rd Uhlan Regiment No. 21, Kaiser Wilhelm II, King of Prussia, in Chemnitz, founded in 1905; in parade form.

226 Württemberg: Officer's chapka in post-1897 form, for officers of the King Wilhelm I Uhlan Regiment (2nd Württemberg) No. 20, of Ludwigsburg; in parade form, but without a hair plume.

227 Prussia: Chapka for officers of the 3rd Uhlan Guard Regiment of Potsdam, in parade form. This model with hooked facings was introduced in 1868, and worn in this elegant form as of 1897. The parade facings followed the usual color scheme of the old army: white, red, yellow and light blue (for regiments 1, 2, 3 and 4, etc.).

228 Prussia: Chapka for enlisted men of the Count Haeseler Uhlan Regiment (2nd Brandenburg) No. 11, of Saarburg, in the form worn around 1910. A typically robust museum piece.

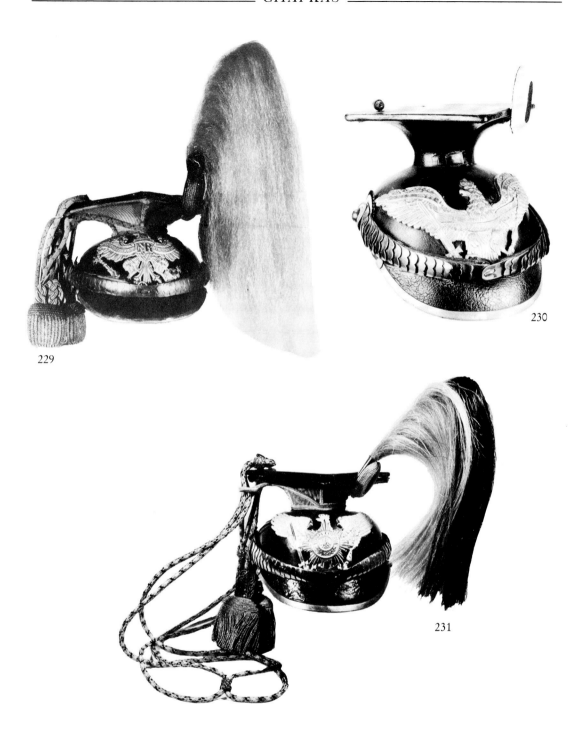

229

230

231

229 Prussia: Officer's chapka of Uhlan Regiment 11 in parade form; circa 1912.

230 Prussia: Chapka for enlisted men of the Grand Duke Friedrich of Baden (Rhenish) Uhlan Regiment No. 7 of Saarbrücken. This regiment was awarded the silvered grenadier eagle (guard eagle without a star) in 1913.

231 Prussia: Chapka for sergeants of the (3rd) Uhlan Guards, in parade form, circa 1910. The sergeants of the guard had a special silver and black twisted restraining cord with silver fringe, differing from the usual one for non-commissioned officers. Guard star on the eagle, without enamel.

232

233

234

232 Prussia: Chapka for non-commissioned Uhlan Guard officers, parade form, circa 1910, with generally prescribed restraining cord of white wool shot with black.

233 Prussia: Substitute for an Uhlan chapka, made of felt, 1915.

234 Prussia: Wartime version of an Uhlan Guard chapka with removable metal top and field gray trim with chinstrap, 1915.

239 Prussia: Officer's fur cap, M/1850, from the Pomeranian Hussar Regiment No. 5 (Blücher's Hussars), of Stolp. Brown otter fur with hawk-feather parade plume. Worn until 1860, then a national bandeau was added. As of 1866 new fur caps, without the front and rear peaks, were introduced.

240 Hannover: Fur cap for enlisted men of the Hussar Guard Regiment, 1856-1866. Black sealskin with yellow bandeau reading "PENINSULA-WATERLOO-EL BODON." yellow and white hair plume, red Kolpak.

241 Prussia: Fur cap for officers of the von Schill (1st Silesian) Hussar Regiment No. 4, of Ohlau. Low form, as was the style circa 1880-1890. Brown otter fur, gilded bandeau and lemon-yellow Kolpak.

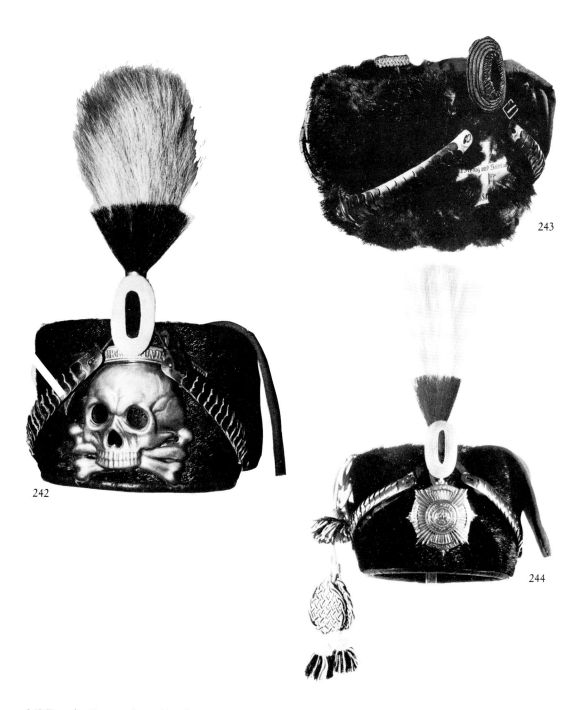

242 Prussia: Fur cap for enlisted men of the 1st Life Guard Hussar Regiment No. 1, of Danzig-Langfuhr, with parade plume (standing since 1903, previously hanging). The two Life Guard Hussar Regiments had a round arched national bandeau, different in form from those of the other regiments.

243 Prussia: Fur cap of a reserve officer in Count Goetzen's (2nd Silesian) Hussar Regiment No. 6 of Leobschütz and Ratibor, post-1897. Reserve officers removed the bandeau and wore the home guard cross (here gilded). Red Kolpak.

244 Prussia: Fur cap for non-commissioned officers of the Life Guard Hussar Regiment, post-1903. With the fancy-dress decoration worn for parades, plus a restraining cord.

245 Braunschweig: Fur cap for officers of Hussar Regiment No. 17, service uniform. This regiment had special chains for officers, a cover of black bearskin, and a death's-head emblem under the bandeau, which read "PENINSULA-SICILIEN-WATERLOO-MARS LA TOUR." Worn in this form as of 1873 or 1897.

246 Saxony: Fur cap for reserve officers in the King Albert Hussar Regiment No. 18, of Grossenhain, post-1897 form. The Saxon reserve officers wore the home guard cross under the emblem on the star. Red Kolpak.

247 Prussia: Fur cap for enlisted men of the King Wilhelm I (1st Rhenish) Hussar Regiment No. 7, of Bonn. This regiment was the only one to have a monogram on the fur cap, which was awarded in 1861 and still retained the "I" after 1888.

249 Imperial Germany: Tropical helmet for officers of the protective troops, M/1889/97, worn with daytime and mess uniforms, with gilded trim.

250-251 Imperial Germany: Shako for enlisted men of the telegraph and training battalions of the protective troops. Imitation of a leather shako in tropical form (cork with khaki cloth covering); the rear brim folds up so as not to hinder head movement. Picture 251 shows the same shako with a neck protector hooked on.

252 Imperial Germany: Tropical helmet for the East Asian Expeditionary Corps in China, M/1901, worn with the summer uniform (a pointed helmet in the winter). Also used by the protective troops in Africa.

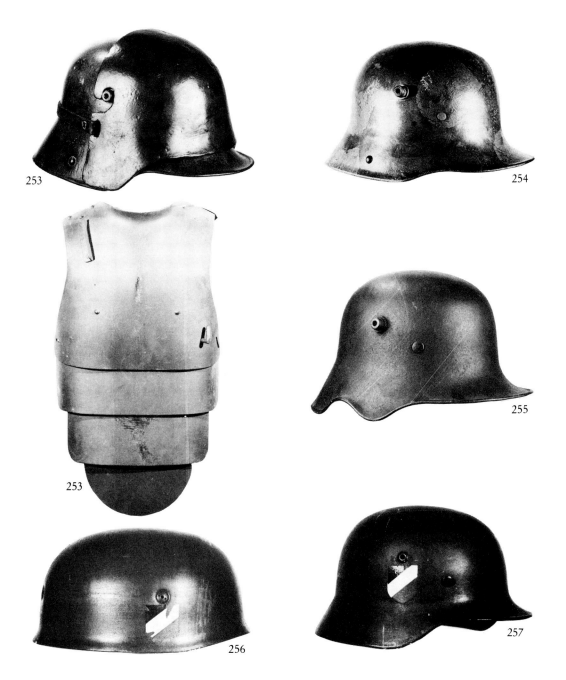

253 Imperial Germany: Steel helmet, M/1916, with additional front plate to protect against shrapnel effect on the front lines, usually worn along with the illustrated "trench armor." Clearly similar to the sappers' armor of the Thirty Years' War and the 19th Century.

254 Imperial Germany: Steel helmet, M/1916, with which the troops were gradually equipped as of the end of February 1916. The old M/91 chinstraps were used at first.

255 Imperial Germany: Steel helmet, M/1918, with ear cutouts, for radio troops and artillery, developed in the summer of 1918, later called the "cavalry steel helmet."

256 German Reich: Steel helmet for paratroopers ("Parachute riflemen"), M/1938.

257 German Reich: Steel helmet, M/1935, for the Wehrmacht, somewhat lighter and better-looking.

Almost no original pieces of 18th-Century and earlier uniforms have been preserved. Pests such as moths and mice have eaten up such textiles as were not simply discarded after use, worn for everyday farm chores, remodeled or used as rags. The clothing collections during the First and Second World Wars have also caused thousands of uniform treasures of all eras to be destroyed, quite apart from the countless losses to bombing, plundering and forced surrender to the victorious powers. In the years after 1945 not much difference was seen between an 1812 uniform of the Wars of Liberation, a service jacket of the Old Army of 1916, or an enlisted man's combat jacket of World War II—uniforms were uniforms, and whatever was a uniform represented militarism in its most despicable form. In view of this, it is downright amazing that any historical uniforms or equipment of times past have survived at all.

Numerous examples are found only from the Imperial era, especially from the 1890-1900 period to the end of World War I. But it would be impossible to build up a really complete collection of Imperial German uniforms today.

The main sources of information on the uniforms of the years before 1870 are generally pictures. These hand-colored pictures are usually copperplates, steel etchings or lithographs. A whole series of excellent works exist, from which a selection of pictures will be shown.

The new technique of photography made it possible, since about the middle of the last century, to preserve and document everything visible for posterity. Early photographs of soldiers, whether enlisted men or officers, were made only infrequently because of the cost in those days. Only as of 1890 did photography become so economical that everyone could afford the luxury. Photographs are documents, better than any drawing (although the photos were often retouched, whether out of vanity or accuracy), and the uniform scholar will sooner or later not be able to get along without this excellent form of uniform documentation.

Thus far, original photographs have attained rather little respect among uniform collectors, and the significance of a photograph is debated, especially as applied to points of disagreement. It is impossible to present a study of uniforms in the manner of a Paul Pietsch, Richard Knötel or Louis Braun. Then too, their works exist. But the following pictures give a basic impression of the uniforms of the various service arms and ranks.

For a better understanding of military history, a look at 19th-Century history is necessary.

In 1806 the old (first) Empire, the Holy Roman Empire of the German Nation, came to an end. Napoleon I enlarged the number of German kingdoms—there were now Prussia, Bavaria, Saxony, Württemberg (the last three as of 1806, Prussia since 1701), plus the Kingdom of Westphalia (which existed only from 1809 to 1813) and Hannover as of 1814. Hesse-Kassel became an electorate in 1803 and was annexed by Prussia in 1866. Baden and Hesse-Darmstadt became grand duchies in 1806, as did Mecklenburg-Schwerin, Mecklenburg-Strelitz and Saxe-Weimar in 1815, with Oldenburg becoming a grand duchy in 1829. There were ten duchies: Braunschweig (1813), Holstein (1815), Nassau (1806), Saxe-Altenburg (1825-26), Saxe-Hildburghausen (in existence since 1683, belonging to Saxe-Meiningen since 1826), Saxe-Coburg-Gotha (1826), Saxe-Meiningen (1826), Anhalt-Dessau, Anhalt-Köthen and Anhalt-Bernburg (all 1807), Lauenburg (1815). Plus ten principalities: Schwarzburg-Sondershausen, Schwarzburg-Rudolstadt, Hohenzollern-Sigmaringen, Hohenzollern-Hechingen, Waldeck,

Pyrmont, the younger and elder lines of Reuss, Schaumburg-Lippe and Lippe-Detmold. Plus four free cities: Hamburg, Bremen, Lübeck and Frankfurt. Out of these larger and a few smaller units, 25 federal states eventually formed the second German Reich in 1871; they numbered four kingdoms, six grand duchies, five duchies, seven principalities and three free cities. Hannover, Frankfurt, Lauenburg, Schleswig-Holstein, Nassau, Electoral Hesse and other small units were annexed by Prussia. Helmets and uniforms from many of the smaller states have been preserved. Independent uniform standards were maintained until 1842-43, after which most of the states adopted the new Prussian uniforms, with Saxony following in 1867, Württemberg in 1871, and Bavaria in stages in 1873, 1886 and 1890. Some of the states rejected the dictated Prussian uniform styles, at least in part: Hannover in 1858 and Nassau in 1862, for instance. After the war of 1866 most German troop units became contingency units of the Royal Prussian Army, especially those of the grand duchies, duchies, principalities and free Hanseatic cities; the constitution of the North German Federation made the King of Prussia the "Federal Commander-in-Chief." The troops of Württemberg and Saxony were numbered as part of the Prussian Army. Only Bavaria maintained its independence in the numbering of its army corps and regiments until 1918. The independent uniforming policy in Saxony (shako) ended in 1867, in Bavaria (service jacket) in 1873 and (crested helmet) 1886, and in Württemberg (service jacket with two rows of buttons) in 1892.

In the 17th Century the uniform consisted of a wide, overcoat-like jacket with wide sleeves and large cuffs, often called a "Kasacke" (or Casaque).

At the beginning of the 18th Century, the uniform coat became slimmer in cut, but was worn open, unbuttoned, as before. Under this uniform coat the soldier wore a shirt with a jacketlike garment over it, as well as knee breeches and hosiery, to which knee-high linen leggings, buttoned at the sides, were added in 1715.

Around the middle of the 18th Century the uniform coat became visibly narrower, and it was already being worn buttoned across the chest. It was said at first that the Prussians made their coats smaller to save money; actually, though, they were just trying to get away from the wide French style. Only after the Seven Years' Wars (1756-1783), when Prussian finances were greatly insufficient because of the restoration of war damage, were uniforms really made smaller to save material. Around 1800 the uniform coat was buttoned down to the waist, and the skirts, which had been cut back for decades already, now began to look like the tails of a frock coat. Around 1800 these tails still reached almost to the knee, but by the time the service jacket was introduced in 1843 they had been shortened to the length of two handbreadths. The coat was closed in front with two vertical rows of buttons.

From the beginning, the Hussars had brought along their typical clothing from Hungary, including the Dolman, a short jacket with cords, and the fur hanging over the shoulder in summer, a Dolman whose edges were decorated with fur.

The cuirassiers already wore a doublet in the 18th Century that was similar to that worn around 1840. But the cuirassiers' doublets were not fastened with buttons, but with hooks and eyes at the front. This method remained unchanged through the years.

The Uhlans originally called their jacket the "Kurtka"; it was the old fancy-dress coat of the Polish lancers, a short service jacket with cords. Other uniform pieces worn in the early 19th Century were the Spencer of the cavalry, a stable jacket that was more simply made, and the Drillich or canvas jacket, likewise worn for stable service. In addition, the Drillich later became the soldier's usual training and work clothing.

The new service jacket introduced in 1842 had a single row of buttons in front, a low collar with rounded corners, and skirts all around. Until the Seventies the skirts were cut to hang like a bell, after which they were worn flat and smooth.

Officers' service dress included the overcoat introduced in 1808, a knee-length service coat with two rows of buttons and lapels. Although it was officially abolished several times, this overcoat was kept until the end of World War I, as it was the most comfortable piece of uniform clothing.

For bad weather, officers and men received heavy coats from 1807 on; until 1888 they were "darkened gray", meaning black; afterward they were gray.

Officers had a Paletot (a coat extending halfway down the thighs), the coat (almost ankle-length) and a sleeveless cloak.

When the service jacket was introduced, the Hussars were given the Attila, a type of uniform coat similar to the service jacket, which was set with (fewer and fewer) rows of cord. There was a difference between the officers' parade and interim Attilas. The first was set with costly embroidery in gold or silver, the latter with simple black and white edging, which gave way in 1884 to a silver edging shot with black (Prussian colors). Fur jackets were worn only by those Hussar regiments who were given them by their princely chiefs. The fur Attila was also called a "Dolman" as of 1842.

The Uhlans originally wore the doublet as did other troops, with two rows of buttons in front. The two chest facings were soon worn buttoned for parades, and the jacket was closed by hooks. As of 1853 the Uhlans' "Ulanka" was introduced in its final form, with two rows of buttons forming a V, onto which a facing of prescribed color was buttoned for parades. As of 1842 the cuirassiers wore the "Koller", a white jacket of coarse woolen cloth (called kersey), which was trimmed around the collar and down the front with piping in the regimental colors and closed by hooks and eyes. The jacket pipings were made of wool for enlisted men and of gold or silver material for officers, to match their buttons.

This is a brief overview of the various types of uniform. The information applies to the Prussian Army but can be applied extensively to the other states. There was previously no typical difference between parade and battle dress. It was Frederick the Great who, for reasons of expense, ordered different parade and combat uniforms for his Life Guard Battalion in 1756. During the Napoleonic Wars of Liberation, the armies still went into the field in their parade uniforms. As of the mid-19th Century the distinction was made, and in 1866 for the first time, field shoulder pieces were worn in the field instead of epaulettes—the epaulettes now became elements of the parade uniform.

258

258 Prussia: Lieutenant in the Brandenburg Cuirassier Regiment (Tsar Nicholas I of Russia),
lithograph by C. Mittag, Berlin 1842. (Immediately before the introduction of the new helmet.)

263

264

263 Prussia: Prince Friedrich Karl of Prussia (1828-1885)in his uniform as 2nd Chief of the 1st Life Guard Hussar Regiment No. 1.

264 Prussia: A major in the Pomeranian Hussar Regiment (Blücher's Hussars) No. 5, of Stolp. Picture taken in 1863. This regiment was the only one to wear a special parade Attila decorated with silver fringe.

265

266

267

265 Prussia: Second Lieutenant von Fürstenberg-Stammheim of the 7th Home Guard Hussar Regiment (Officer of the Cavalry in the 2nd Rhenish Home Guard Regiment No. 28, 3rd Battalion, in Siegburg). In parade uniform on horseback. Picture taken in 1866.

266 Prussia: A second lieutenant of the 9th Home Guard Hussar Regiment (Officer of the Cavalry in the 3rd Rhenish Home Guard Regiment No. 29). Picture taken in 1865.

267 Prussia: Cavalry Captain von Bredow of the 1st Uhlan Guard Regiment, of Potsdam. Picture taken circa 1865.

268

269

268 Prussia: Second Lieutenant Stumm of the 7th Home Guard Regiment (Officer of the Cavalry in the 4th Rhenish Home Guard Regiment No. 30, 2nd Battalion, in Saarlouis). Picture taken in 1866. The officer wears the "foul weather cap" based on an English model. Officially the chapka was to be worn in service with a black oilcloth cover, but for the sake of comfort, chapkas of black leather were worn without eagle emblems, and with the field emblem in the form of a leather flap. Note also the long cloth trousers with leather trim, the so-called "tin trousers."

269 Prussia: A major in the Gardes du Corps Regiment. Parade uniform. Picture taken circa 1867.

270

271

272

273

270 Prussia: A major on the staff of the 2nd Artillery Brigade, picture taken in 1866.

271 Prussia: The colonel of a line infantry regiment, photographed at Königsberg in 1866.

272 Prussia: A sword ensign of the guard infantry, picture taken circa 1865.

273 Braunschweig: A private of Infantry Regiment 92 in a "Polrock", picture taken about 1870.

274

274 Württemberg: Staff officer of the cavalry regiments, picture taken in 1860.

275

275 Bavaria: Crown Prince Ludwig (later King Ludwig II, born 1845, reigned 1864-1886) in the uniform of a first lieutenant of the rifle company of the 1st Infantry Regiment, King. Picture taken circa 1862.

276 Bavaria: Major General of the Cavalry. Picture taken circa 1873. The belt was newly introduced as the identifying mark of an officer, in place of the ring collar.

277 Bavaria: A captain of the 1st Infantry Regiment, King, picture taken circa 1863.

278 Bavaria: A first lieutenant in the 2nd Infantry Regiment, Crown Prince. Picture taken circa 1864, with the helmet just introduced.

279 Bavaria: One-year volunteer in an infantry life guard regiment, picture taken circa 1875.

280

281

282

283

_280_ Bavaria: Rifleman of the 3rd Infantry Regiment "Prince Carl", circa 1865. From 1860 to 1873 the wings on the shoulders were worn without shoulder flaps. The riflemen, like the Jägers, had green braid and a green woolen crest on the helmet (Jäger helmet M/1845).

_281_ Bavaria: Infantryman of the 14th Infantry Regiment of Hartmann in Nürnberg, ready to march into the field, in 1870.

_282_ Bavaria: Artillery lieutenant in parade uniform, circa 1863.

_283_ Bavaria: Corporal of the 4th Artillery Regiment "King", of Augsburg, in parade uniform. Picture taken circa 1875, with the newly introduced service jacket after the Prussian model, and the cuffs of the batteries on foot.

284

285   286

284 Prussia: Cavalry general in parade uniform, mounted, photographed May 2, 1903. The embroidered coat was the general's dress uniform until 1909.

285 Prussia: Cavalry general in the uniform of the Cuirassier Regiment "Queen" (Pomeranian) No. 2, of Pasewalk. Service jacket with ring collar. Picture taken circa 1900. Generals with regimental uniforms wore the regimental uniforms, not the embroidered general's coat, plus epaulettes with stiff braid and the appropriate emblem of the regiment.

286 Prussia: Artillery general in parade uniform (á la suite of the 2nd Lorraine Field Artillery Regiment No. 34, of Metz, with the chain of the Royal Prussian High Order of the Black Eagle). Picture taken circa 1912.

287

287 Bavaria: King Ludwig III (1913-1918) and Queen Therese. The King wears the M/1910 general's uniform (as interim jacket with silver embroidery, introduced as of 1901) with the emblem of a field marshal. Picture taken circa 1914.

288

289

290

291

_288_ Prussia: Surgeon General in service, wearing a parade service jacket. Surgeons wore no belts; the field belt with a special type of buckle was granted them only in 1914. Picture taken circa 1910.

_289_ Bavaria: Lieutenant general in parade uniform. The general's helmet with silvered trim and feather plume, replacing the hat, was introduced in 1902; the enameled central piece of the coat of arms on the helmet came only in 1913. Picture taken circa 1907.

_290_ Saxony: Lieutenant general in parade uniform. The Saxon generals' coats were the only ones in the German Army to have especially ornamented uniform buttons. The feather plume was also unusual, being made solely of white heron feathers, Picture taken circa 1902.

_291_ Prussia: Lieutenant general in service, wearing the interim service jacket. In 1900 this was embellished with the old Larisch embroidery on the collar and cuffs. As of 1909 this jacket replaced the embroidered jacket for parade use too.

292

293

292 Prussia: Oboist of the 1st Foot Guard Regiment, parade uniform with grenadier cap. Picture taken circa 1900. For many years the musicians of the guards wore "swallows' nests" with short silver fringe matching their buttons.

293 Prussia: A major in the Queen Augusta Grenadier Guard Regiment No. 4 of Berlin. Service jacket with gold embroidery; the special sword of this regiment, which the officers received in 1886 on the 25th anniversary of Empress and Queen Augusta as chief of the regiment, is clear to see. Picture taken circa 1900.

294   295

294 Prussia: A sergeant of Railroad Regiment No. 1, of Berlin. Prescribed uniform with M/1889 sword on a black lacquered leather belt. The patterned braid of guard non-commissioned officers is easy to recognize. Picture taken circa 1905.

295 Prussia: Prince Oskar of Prussia (5th son of Kaiser Wilhelm II, 1888-1958) as a captain with the uniform of the King Wilhelm I Grenadier Regiment (2nd West Prussian) No. 7, of Liegnitz. Most of the twelve grenadier regiments had special embroidery on the collars and cuffs of their service jackets. The prince wears the mass uniform.

296

297

296 Bavaria: A lieutenant of the 2nd Infantry Regiment "Crown Prince", in parade uniform. The Bavarian infantry had no parade plumes on their helmets. Picture taken in 1910.

297 Bavaria: One-year volunteer of the 13th Infantry Regiment "Kaiser Franz Joseph of Austria, King of Hungary", of Ingolstadt. In ordnance uniform, picture taken in 1912. One-year volunteers had to serve only one year instead of two, but had to pay all their expenses themselves.

298

299

300

301

298 Hesse-Darmstadt: One-year volunteer of Life Guard Infantry Regiment (1st Grand Ducal Hessian) No. 115, of Darmstadt, in ordnance uniform, circa 1910.

299 Hesse-Darmstadt: First lieutenant of the Kaiser Wilhelm Infantry Regiment (2nd Grand Ducal Hessian) No. 116, of Giessen. Mess uniform, with the open bottom button of the sleeve panel clear to see. Picture taken circa 1900.

300 Prussia: Colonel and Commander of the 6th Thuringian Infantry Regiment No. 95, of Gotha-Hildburghausen-Coburg, in an overcoat; this was the officers' favorite piece of clothing for daily service. Picture taken circa 1910.

301 Prussia: Reserve lieutenant of the 2nd Lower Alsatian Infantry Regiment No. 137, of Hagenau. Parade uniform. His stately appearance must have amused his contemporary viewers too. Picture taken in 1908.

303

302

304

302 Bavaria: Infantryman of the 15th Infantry Regiment "King Friedrich August III of Saxony." of Neuburg on the Danube, ready for the field, with rolled overcoat over his pack and 98 rifle. Picture taken circa 1905.

303 Prussia: Sergeant of Infantry Regiment Landgrave Friedrich I of Hesse-Kassel (1st Electoral Hessian) No. 81, of Frankfurt am Main, in Class A uniform with second class marksman's cord. Picture taken circa 1912.

304 Saxony: Grenadier of the 1st (Life Guard) Grenadier Regiment No. 100, of Dresden, in (winter) parade uniform for going to church, thus without a rifle, cartridge case or bayonet. Helmet with nonstandard buffalo-hair plume instead of horsehair. Picture taken circa 1912.

305

306

305 Prussia: Lieutenant of the Jäger Guard Battalion of Potsdam, in Mess Uniform, picture taken circa 1905.

306 Prussia: Sergeant of Home Guard Inspection, Berlin, in Class A uniform, picture taken circa 1900.

307

308

309

307 Prussia: Rifleman of the Guard Rifle Batallion, Berlin-Lichterfelde, in a Litewka, with the King's Prize (company marksmanship decoration) on the right sleeve. Picture taken circa 1900.

308 Bavaria: Jäger of the 1st Jäger Battalion "King", of Freising. Picture taken circa 1910.

309 Saxony: Corporal of the Prince Georg Rifle (Fusilier) Regiment No. 108, of Dresden, wearing Class A uniform and overcoat. This regiment wore a shako like that of the Saxon Jägers, plus a special belt buckle with the crowned monogram "G." Picture taken circa 1912.

311

310

312

310 Prussia: Garde du Corps in full-dress watch uniform, picture taken circa 1910. The matte white silvered parade eagle on the helmet is easy to see.

311 Prussia: Guard cuirassier in parade uniform, with cuirass. Picture taken circa 1914.

312 Prussia: Cuirassier of Cuirassier Regiment Tsar Nicholas I of Russia (Brandenburg) No. 6, of Brandenburg. This regiment also had tombac helmets, as did the guards. The manner of wearing the bandolier is clear to see. Picture taken circa 1912.

313

314

313 Prussia: First lieutenant of the Gardes du Corps Regiment in full-dress watch uniform, with the red cloth outer vest with silver embroidered star and edging on the jacket, worn until 1900, plus the bandolier normally worn is service. After 1900 the outer vest of red velvet with lavish embroidered edging was worn, as well as the bandolier. Compare the color picture on the dust jacket.

314 Prussia: Lieutenant in the Cuirassier Regiment von Driessen (Westphalian) No. 4, of Münster, in parade uniform with cuirass. Picture taken circa 1910. The long projecting epaulettes are easy to see; they had especially long extenders, so the cuirass would not lie over them.

315

316

315 Prussia: Lieutenant Colonel á la suite of the Gardes du Corps Regiment, in parade uniform, mounted. Behind him is a general of the cavalry. Picture taken circa 1910.

316 Saxony: Kettledrummer of the Carbine Regiment (2nd Heavy Regiment) of Borna, near Leipzig, with parade kettledrum banners; next to him is the Chief Music Master of the regiment, mounted. Picture taken in 1912.

317

318

319

320

317 Bavaria: First lieutenant of the 1st Cuirassier Regiment "Prince Carl of Bavaria", in parade uniform, picture taken circa 1870.

318 Bavaria: Corporal of the 1st Heavy Cavalry Regiment "Prince Carl of Bavaria", of Munich, in parade uniform with marksman's cord first class. In 1879 the Bavarian cuirassiers were changed to heavy cavalry and ultimately took on the appearance of dragoons in the Prussian model. Picture taken in 1912.

319 Saxony: First lieutenant of the Cavalry Guard Regiment (1st Heavy Regiment), of Dresden, in an overcoat with peaked cap. The aircraft observer emblem is also visible. Picture taken in 1917; the officer is just 19 years old.

320 Saxony: Cavalryman of the Carbine Regiment, in orderly uniform. In 1879 the Saxon heavy cavalry were given the Prussian-type cuirassier helmet. The picture, taken circa 1910, clearly shows the cuirassier helmet M/1889-94.

321

322

321 Prussia: Lieutenant of the Life Guard Hussar Regiment, Potsdam, in parade uniform; picture taken in 1899. The special full-dress pendant on the fur cap and the "Schnoitasch" of the full-dress trousers are clear to see.

322 Prussia: Non-commissioned officer of the 2nd Life Guard Hussar Regiment No. 2, of Danzig-Langfuhr, in orderly uniform; picture taken circa 1905.

392

393

394

395

39

397

Prussian Officers' Cartridge Cases, circa 1914:

392 Guard Cavalry

393 Gardes du Corps Regiment, for full-dress watch uniform (since 1900)

394 Life Guard Cuirassier Regiment (since 1902)

395 Queen's Cuirassier Regiment

396 Mounted Grenadier Regiment No. 3 (since 1897)

397 King's Mounted Jäger Regiment No. 1 (since 1905)

398

399

400

401

402

403

398 Prussia: Field-gray infantry helmet, 1915. Substitute material of cork covered with cloth, brass trim, chinstrap with simplified attachment, length adjustment as with the chinstrap of the peaked cap.

399 German Empire: Field-gray shako of the sea battalions, substitute material, 1915. Felt pressed in one piece, with chinstrap on M/91 button.

400 Baden: Pair of epaulettes of a senior general with the rank of field marshal (as Chief of the 1st Baden Life Guard Grenadier Regiment, No. 109, of Karlsruhe), post-1911.

401 Baden: Pair of epaulettes of a senior general with the rank of field marshal (as Chief of the Royal Prussian Uhlan Regiment "Grand Duke Friedrich of Baden" (Rhenish) No. 7, of Saarbrücken), pre-1911.

402 Bavaria: Pair of epaulettes of a senior general with the rank of field marshal, pre-1904.

403 Saxony: Pair of epaulettes of a general of the infantry as chief of the Rifle (Fusilier) Regiment "Prince Georg" No. 108, of Dresden, circa 1888.

404 405

406 407

404-407 Reprints from the *History of the Castle Guard Company of His Majesty the Kaiser and King 1829-1909*, by Leo von Pfanneberg, Berlin, 1909.
The plates show clearly the splendor that was given to court troops, the development of uniform styles, and especially the fondness of 19th-Century Prussian kings for the uniforms of the glorious era of Frederick the Great. Kaiser Wilhelm II in particular had numerous court celebrations in historical costumes of Frederick's day.

408

409

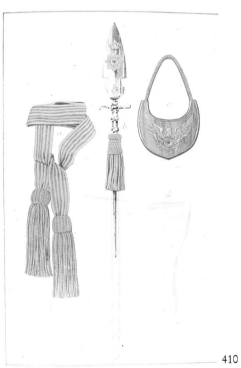

410

411

408-411 Further uniform plates from the "History of the Castle Guard Company." This series of pictures is among the best illustrations to be found in Prussian regimental histories.

412

412 Bavaria: Life Guards of the Halberdiers in the uniform worn until 1852, which much resembled uniforms worn for centuries. The coat, a "Cassaque" after a Spanish model, which was worn with the full dress uniform, is especially notable. For service the Halberdiers had worn a doublet (Kollet) to the army pattern since the beginning of the 19th Century.
Colored lithograph by Gustav Kraus, circa 1840.

413   414   415

_413-415_ Bavaria: Halberdiers in full dress uniforms with outer vest, helmet with added lion, and Cuise.

416

417

418

_417_ Bavaria: Halberdier in full dress uniform (minus carbine). Picture dated ''Christmas 1911.''

_416, 418_ Bavaria: Original uniform of a halberdier in full dress, pre-1888, still with the M/1839 percussion carbine. Front and rear views.

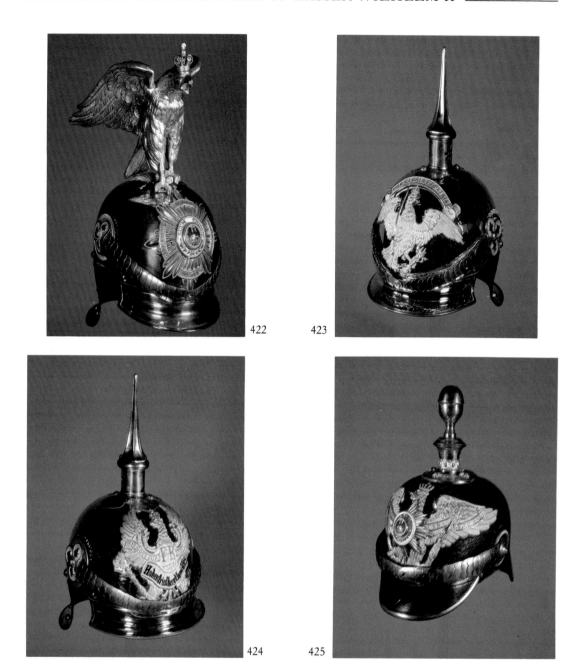

Helmets Owned by Kaiser Wilhelm II:

422 Officer's helmet of the Royal Prussian Gardes du Corps with parade eagle. The Kaiser's favorite helmet.

423 Officer's helmet of the Life Guard Cuirassier Regiment "Great Elector" (Silesian) No. 1, with the "Frederician" eagle introduced in 1902. This regiment was one of the Kaiser's four life guard regiments.

424 Officer's helmet of the Queen's Cuirassier Regiment (Pomeranian) No. 2, of Pasewalk. Wilhelm II was, of course, not the chief of this regiment, but it was one of his favorite regiments, and he placed his son, Crown Prince Wilhelm, à la suite of this regiment.

425 Officer's helmet of the 1st Field Artillery Guard Regiment, Berlin.

427

426

428

Helmets Owned by Kaiser Wilhelm II

426 Officer's chapka of the King's Uhlan Regiment (1st Hannover) No. 13, of Hannover. With the extremely rare special parade plume of heron feathers, which only regimental chiefs could wear.

427 Officer's shako of the Machine-Gun Guard Unit No. 1, of Potsdam. Likewise a troop unit of which the Kaiser was not the chief.

428 Officer's helmet of the 1st Foot Guard Regiment, with ''Semper Talis'' bandeau. This regiment was also known as the ''most splendid regiment in Christendom.'' Since many years before, the King of Prussia was the chief of this regiment, and all Prussian princes became lieutenants in the regiment at the age of ten.

429

430

431

432

429 Service jacket M/1915 of the 1st Foot Guard Regiment (so-called ''Future Peacetime Uniform''), with leather belt and special field buckle worn only by the Kaiser, and peaked cap. The Kaiser's left arm was withered from birth, thus his uniforms can be recognized at once.

430 Litewka M/1915 of the Guard Rifle Battalion, with peaked cap. The open lapels, lined with green velvet, are a special feature that the Kaiser allowed himself.

431 Service jacket M/1915 from the Gaurdes du Corps Regiment, with peaked cap. The Kaiser was Protector of the Royal Prussian Order of St. John and wore the order's cloth cross on every uniform.

432 Attila M/1915 of the 1st Life Guard Hussar Regiment No. 1, with peaked cap.

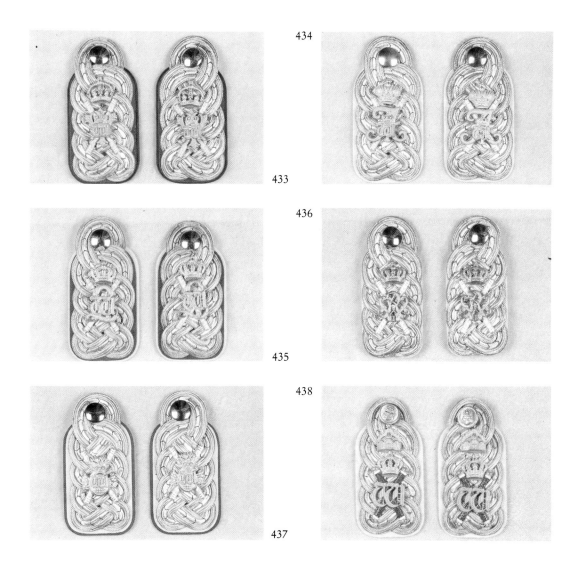

433 Pair of shoulder pieces of Kaiser Wilhelm II, in post-1915 form, for the uniform of the 1st Dragoon Guard Regiment "Queen Victoria of Great Britain and Ireland", in Berlin. Along with a field marshal's emblem, the Kaiser always wore the monogram of his grandfather, Kaiser Wilhelm I, whose flank adjutant he was, as well as the monogram worn by the regiment. According to regulations, two crowns were never to be worn simultaneously, but even the Kaiser's shoulder pieces show variations, as can be seen here.

434 Pair of shoulder pieces for the uniform of the Tsar Alexander Grenadier Guard Regiment No. 1, Berlin, post-1915.

435 Pair of shoulder pieces for the uniform of the Queen's (Pomeranian) Cuirassier Regiment No. 2, of Pasewalk, post-1915.

436 Pair of shoulder pieces for the uniform of the Royal Saxon 2nd Grenadier Regiment No. 101, "Kaiser Wilhelm, King of Prussia", of Dresden, post-1915.

437 Pair of shoulder pieces for the uniform of the 1st Field Artillery Guard Regiment, Berlin, Mobile Unit, post-1915.

438 Pair of shoulder pieces for the uniform of an Admiral of the Imperial Navy, with enameled admiral's emblem, post-1915.

439

439 A look at one of the Kaiser's uniform closets at Haus Doorn.

440

441

442

Officers' Gifts for Kaiser Wilhelm II

440, 442 Grenadier officer's cap of the 1st Foot Guard Regiment; unfolded, it shows the portraits of the Kings of Prussia and the Imperial Family as of 1894. In the eighth oval is the dedication: "For the 25th Officers' Anniversary of His Majesty the Emperor and King Wilhelm II, February 9, 1894." Presently at Haus Doorn, Holland.

441 Silver statue portraying a flag-bearer of Frederick the Great's Guard Battalion. The Kaiser's military career is traced in gold lettering on the red marble base. Gift of the officers of the 1st Guard Regiment on May 3, 1900, when Wilhelm II took the rank of Field Marshal.

Four officers' portraits

443 Bavaria: Captain of the 2nd Infantry Regiment "Electoral Prince", Munich, 1789-1800. The Rumford uniform system was complex; the rank of an officer could be told by the number of buttonholes and their braid edging on the lapels.

444 Prussia: Officer of Musketeer Regiment 34, circa 1806, with the Pour le Mérite medal. The officer's belt was worn over the coat, which was fastened to the waist, as of February 1805.

445 Bavaria: Captain of the 11th Infantry Regiment "Kinkel", garrisoned at Landsberg and Kempten, circa 1812.

446 Bavaria: Lieutenant of the 1st Light Cavalry Regiment "Crown Prince" of Nürnberg and Bayreuth, circa 1840.

455

454

_454-455_ Prussia: Two precisely made uniforms for children, probably for sons of ruling houses. At left, the uniform of a lieutenant of the Life Guard Hussars, at right the uniform of a lieutenant in the Gardes du Corps Regiment. Height of the figures: approximately 140 cm.

467

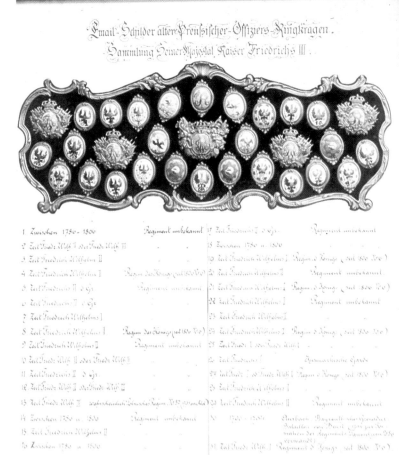

468

Prussia: former collection of Emperor Friedrich III (1888):

467-468 Collection of enameled emblems from 18th-Century Prussian ring collars. Last owned by Kaiser Wilhelm II, now at the Huis Doorn Museum, Holland. Includes a facsimile of the original description of the collection.

323

324

323 Saxony: Colonel Carl Eduard, Duke of Saxe-Coburg-Gotha, à la suite of the 1st Hussar Regiment "King Albert" No. 18, of Grossenhain. The picture, taken circa 1908, shows the Duke in parade uniform, mounted. The regiment had no fur jackets, but a fur jacket was prescribed for regimental chiefs and officers, the fur not being of the usual gray lamb, but rather sable fur.

324 Prussia: Officer of the 2nd Westphalian Hussar Regiment No. 11 in Krefeld, in undress service uniform with button coat, without shoulder pieces, which was non-regulation. Picture taken circa 1900.

325

325 Prussia: Retired major of the 2nd Uhlan Guard Regiment in an overcoat (undress service uniform). Under the shoulder pieces the herringbone pattern of the braid for retired officers can be seen. Picture taken circa 1905.

326

327

326 Prussia: Member of the Hennig von Treffenfeld Uhlan Regiment (Altmark) No. 16, of Salzwedel-Gardelegen. Parade uniform, picture taken circa 1914. The especially high-quality cut of the self-owned Ulanka is noteworthy.

327 Prussia: Non-commissioned officer of the 1st Uhlan Guard Regiment of Potsdam. Parade uniform, with the non-regulation but typical way of wearing the rolled-up restraining cord on the facings. On the right sleeve are three chevrons, awarded for lance fighting. Picture taken circa 1905.

328

329

328 Bavaria: Lieutenant of the 2nd Uhlan Regiment "King", of Ansbach, in parade uniform. Picture taken circa 1905.

329 Bavaria: Kettledrummer of the 1st Uhlan Regiment "Kaiser Wilhelm, King of Prussia", of Bamberg, with interim drum banners. Picture taken in 1909.

330

331

332

330 Prussia: Dragoon of the 1st Dragoon Guard Regiment "Queen Victoria of Great Britain and Ireland", of Berlin. Parade uniform with overcoat worn as a cape; semaphore flagman's emblem on the right sleeve.

331 Württemberg: Dragoon of the Queen Olga Dragoon Regiment (1st Württemberg) No. 25 of Ludwigsburg, in parade uniform. Picture taken circa 1910.

332 Hesse-Darmstadt: Corporal of Life Guard Dragoon Regiment (2nd Grand Ducal Hessian) No, 24 of Darmstadt, in Class A uniform, picture taken circa 1912.

333

334

333 Baden: Lieutenant of the 1st Baden Life Guard Dragoon Regiment No. 20 of Karlsruhe, in service uniform, but with non-regulation sword-belt instead of the field belt. Picture taken circa 1900.

334 Württemberg: Colonel Ernst, Prince of Saxe-Weimar, à la suite of the Queen Olga Dragoon Regiment (1st Württemberg) No. 25. Picture taken in 1906.

335

336

335 Bavaria: First lieutenant of the 1st Light Cavalry Regiment "Tsar Nicholas of Russia" of Nürnberg, in parade uniform, picture taken in 1907. Note the nonstandard officer's sword, not the normal M/1890 type but patterned after the M/1889 Prussian infantry officer's sword.

336 Bavaria: Non-commissioned officer of the 2nd Light Cavalry Regiment "Taxis", in parade uniform, picture taken circa 1910.

338

337

337 Bavaria: Captain of the 3rd Light Cavalry Regiment "Duke Karl Theodor", of Dieuze, in an overcoat with peaked cap. Picture taken circa 1905.

338 Bavaria: Captain and Regimental Adjutant of the 4th Light Cavalry Regiment "King", of Augsburg. Service uniform, with the adjutant's belt worn over the shoulder (adjutants did not wear a cartridge case with a bandolier). Picture taken circa 1891.

339

341

340

342

339 Prussia: One-year volunteer in Mounted Jäger Regiment No. 4 of Graudenz. Class A uniform, picture taken in 1913. The mounted Jäger were the newest arm of the German Army. There were thirteen regiments, founded between 1905 and 1913.

340 Prussia: Colonel of the Mounted Jäger Regiment No. 13 of Saarlouis, with medal of an order from World War I (plus Order of Pour le Mérite). Picture taken in 1938.

341 Prussia: Mounted Jäger of Regiment No. 2, of Langensalza, in Class A uniform, picture taken circa 1910.

342 Saxony: Non-commissioned officer of the Royal Saxon Mounted Jäger Squadron, 1900. Before the "mounted Jäger" regiments were organized, individual "mounted Jäger" squadrons existed in the kingdoms, mainly providing orderly and courier service.

343   344

_343_ Prussia: First lieutenant of the 1st Field Artillery Guard Regiment of Berlin, in parade uniform, picture taken circa 1900. The officer wears the "Centenary Medal", given to all officers in the army in 1897 in memory of the 100th birthday of Kaiser Wilhelm I (born March 22, 1797).

_344_ Baden: Major in the Field Artillery Regiment "Grand Duke" (1st Baden) No. 14 of Karlsruhe, in parade uniform. Picture taken in 1912.

345

346   347

345 Bavaria: Cannoneer of the 3rd Field Artillery Regiment "Queen Mother" of Munich. Picture taken circa 1895. Helmet with parade plume, M/1892 side arms on the belt. Bandolier left off, non-regulation.

346 Bavaria: Lieutenant of the 5th Field Artillery Regiment "King Alfonso XIII" of Landau, in service uniform, but with a sword-belt. Picture taken circa 1910.

347 Bavaria: Cannoneer of the 1st Field Artillery Regiment "Prince Regent Luitpold" in parade uniform. Picture taken circa 1910. Yet the artilleryman is obviously wearing a (dress-type) service jacket that must have been made circa 1880-90.

348

349

350

348 Bavaria: Supply train soldier of the 1st Train Battalion, of Munich, in parade uniform. Picture taken circa 1905. Note the heavy, orderly-type M/1826 cavalry saber.

349 Bavaria: Supply train soldier of the 3rd Train Battalion, of Fürth. Parade uniform, typical self-owned uniform plus light self-owned saber. Picture taken circa 1910.

350 Bavaria: Military official (Senior Engineer of Inspection at the Technical Institute) in service uniform, circa 1900.

351

352

351 Prussia: Colonel and Commander of Railroad Regiment No. 2, of Berlin, in parade service jacket. Picture taken circa 1900.

352 Bavaria: Lieutenant of the 1st Engineer Battalion, of Munich, in service uniform. Picture taken in the autumn of 1914.

353

354

355

356

353 German Empire: One-year volunteer of the Naval Infantry, 1st Sea Battalion, of Kiel, in orderly uniform (winter) with overcoat. Picture taken in 1904.

354 German Empire: Imperial Navy, Sea Captain in dress uniform. Picture taken in 1911.

355 German Empire: Naval Infantry. Sea soldier of the 3rd Sea Battalion, of Tsingtau, in summer coat with tropical helmet. Picture taken in 1908.

356 German Empire: Imperial Protective Troops for Southwest Africa. Non-commissioned officer in Class A uniform. The Southwest Africa Medal for fighting men with two battle stars, and the service medal bar under it, are clear to see. Picture taken circa 1910.

357 Prussia: Cadet of the Chief Cadet Institute, Berlin-Lichterfelde. Picture taken circa 1890.

358 Bavaria: Cadet of the Cadet House in Munich. Picture taken circa 1870.

359 Prussia: Cadet as personal page, picture taken circa 1910. Only noble cadets of the Chief Cadet Institute were chosen for the Page Corps; they provided service at full-dress banquets at court, served at the festivals of the High Order of the Black Eagle and similar formal events.

360 Bavaria: Pages in full-dress court uniform, circa 1905. The most important appearances of the Bavarian cadets were their participation in the St. George's Knights' Festival and the Corpus Christi procession in Munich.

361

362

361 Prussia: First Lieutenant of the Grenadier Guard Regiment No. 5, of Spandau, in the M/1910 field uniform. Note the regulation way of wearing the helmet with chinstrap on 91 button. (Instead of the chinstrap, chains were worn on M/91 buttons covered with rosettes for parades).

362 Bavaria: Staff of the Bavarian Infantry Regiment No. 30 in April of 1917. Note the varying uniform details: 2 officers already wear the Bavarian medal bar on the collar, introduced in 1916; trousers vary from long trousers to high boots to high-top shoes and wrapped leggings. The officer at right, in the uniform of the Infantry Life Guard Regiment, wears the regulation side arms on an officer's sword-belt.

364

363

365

363 Prussia: Private of the Gardes du Corps Regiment in field-gray M/1910 service jacket, helmet with field-gray cloth cover. Picture taken September 23, 1914.

364 Prussia: Reserve Lieutenant of the Mansfeld Field Artillery Regiment No. 75, Halle on the Saale, in M/1910 uniform, with peacetime paletot. Picture taken in October of 1914, with the just-awarded Iron Cross Second Class.

365 Prussia: Rifleman of the Rifle Guard Battalion, of Berlin-Lichterfelde. Equipped for the field in August of 1914, with Red Cross armband. Marked on the back: The picture shows me when I left; I still weighed 210 pounds then, and today (1918) just 169. That was a fine weight-loss program.''

366

367

368

366 Württemberg: Wartime wedding, March 1915. Non-commissioned engineer officer with field-gray helmet.

367 Prussia: Army chaplain in the soutane that resembled a service jacket, picture taken circa 1915.

368 Prussia: Two brothers in Home Guard uniforms. The black oilcloth caps with the Home Guard cross much resembled the headgear of the Wars of Liberation. Picture taken circa 1915.

"National Guards" or "Home Guards" did not come into being during the days of uprisings against Napoleon's oppression of Europe, even though a superficial look at history could lead one to think so. Blücher's comment, "Always guard your homeland; I hear much good of it," did, though, encourage the formation of many volunteer corps and home guards in the German states, especially in Prussia.

The farmers' "duty to the state" already led to regional defense in the 17th and 18th Centuries, though not to offensive action. Toward the end of the 18th Century, most of the larger German cities had already formed home guards, which naturally lacked an overall organization, training, uniforming and weaponry.

An example is the "National Guard" founded in 1807 in Bavaria through a thoroughgoing order and divided into three classes. According to their suitability for warfare and fighting ability, those men who were to form the reserve battalions of the regular army were assigned to National Guard First Class, and their service could include duty outside the state boundary. The National Guard Second Class was only put into service in times of real danger inside the state, while the National Guard Third Class just amounted to a statewide unified group of the already existing home guards in the individual cities. At the same time, precise uniform regulations were made, which could only be met partially because of the privation prevailing in the years after Napoleon's rule. Only in the long period of peace after 1815 was it possible to uniform the troops according to regulations. The uniforms of the Bavarian Home Guard until 1848 have already been documented thoroughly in several works. In 1848 the uniforms of the Home Guard were changed thoroughly; the introduction of the Prussian "Pickelhaube" is especially noteworthy, as it had been rejected resoundingly in military circles elsewhere. The following pictures give an impression of the newly introduced Home Guard uniforms, which gave a preview of the uniforms that, following the Prussian model, were used in the active army only 20 to 30 years later.

It is noteworthy that there were no regional home guards in Prussia; the Prussian organizational system since 1808 was so thoroughgoing that, what with the military defense structure existing in the country, home guards were superfluous. In Saxony too there was no actual military organization of the citizenry, while in Württemberg there were regional home guards. There were many home guards in the smaller states, as well as in the free cities.

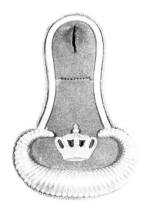 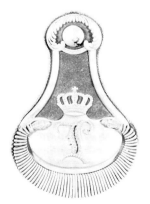 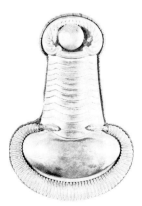

Bavaria: Home Guard epaulettes, 1820, 1825 and 1848.

369 Bavaria: Shako M/1826 for fusilier officers of the Home Guard, with silver pendants and green "Huppe" (emblem of the 4th Battalion).

370 Bavaria: Helmet M/1848 for enlisted men of the Home Guard fusilier battalions. The trim is made of tin. Worn in this form until 1863, thereafter with a black hair plume.

371 Bavaria: Shako M/1826 for cannoneers of the Home Guard artillery, with red pendant and feather plume.

372 Bavaria: Shako M/1826 for Home Guard fusiliers.

373 Bavaria: Helmet M/1848 of the Home Guard of the city of Wasserburg on the Inn, with service spike. City home guards could wear their city's coat of arms as an emblem.

375

376

377

378

375 Bavaria: First Lieutenant of Grenadiers in the Munich Home Guard, in service jacket with draped paletot. At right is the bearskin cap which only grenadier battalions were allowed to wear. Picture taken circa 1860.

376 Bavaria: Sergeant of the Home Guard Fusiliers or Riflemen, picture taken circa 1865. Note the home guard artillery M/1840 with lion's head, worn on the bandolier.

377 Bavaria: First Lieutenant-Surgeon of the Home Guard, with the 1866 memorial cross for civilian doctors.

378 Bavaria: Captain of the Altötting Home Guard, photographed circa 1865. Older gentlemen also appeared proudly in their uniforms.

The present day is sober and purely utilitarian. A part of the uniform worn just for decoration will not find acceptance today—or will it? It is surely an undeniable fact that man decorates himself with everything possible—and sometimes impossible.

Many elements of equipment from olden days have an origin that can be found in the tradition of that service arm, that section of the troops or even an episode in a battle.

A particularly interesting piece of equipment is the Hussar's 'Sabre-Tache'; by the 18th Century it was already a completely useless, purely decorative item that no Hussar wanted to do without, even in World War I. The origin of the saber sheath can be found in the arrow quiver of the Hussars, the oldest organized mounted troops, whose first units already existed in the 15th Century. Even then, the quivers were richly decorated and even regarded as a status symbol or mark of honor. Over the years their type of weapons changed, and the quiver now became a mere piece of decoration, worn on a strap around the body. This origin explains the form of the saber sheath, decorative to the end. Later uses or, more accurately, suggested uses as a "courier's pouch" are only attempts to explain this piece of equipment and have no basis in fact. Because of their decorative ornamentation, saber sheaths are beautiful collectors' items.

Among the mounted troops, the cartridge case was worn on a bandolier when in service, as well as when on parade, until the end of the monarchy. This bullet pouch, hung over the left shoulder, has also been called a "courier's pouch" by the layman. Actually, though, it is a cartridge case, which was carried in earlier times by all troops, and later became a purely decorative item for parade use by officers on account of changed weapons and ammunition technology, while the enlisted men still carried their bullets in a shoulder or belt case until World War I. Naturally, the covers of these bullet pouches were handy places for decorations and coats of arms, so that cartridge cases have become a fascinating subject for collecting.

Strictly speaking, epaulettes and shoulder pieces are not pieces of equipment, but rather insignia of rank, but because of their great variety, they cannot easily be separated from the subject of uniforms. Above all, epaulettes and shoulder pieces (called "Achselklappen" rather than "Schulterstücke" when worn by enlisted men) offered the possibility of presenting the identifying marks of individual regiments visibly. Shoulder flaps originated as a way to prevent the shoulder straps of saber belts or bullet pouches from slipping off. The epaulettes go back to the shoulder protection of medieval armor, and so were originally a protection against cutting weapons. In the 18th Century and the first half of the 19th, epaulettes were often strengthened with chains or metal scales as protection (in Bavaria until 1873, among the Hessian dragoons until 1918); after 1800, epaulettes generally served only a mark of rank, without any protective function. The ring collar is a relic of the neck protection of knightly armor, and served in the end as the mark of an officer. The last example was the ring collar ("Hausse-Col") of the Bavarian Army, which was replaced by the "Schärpe" belt as an identifying mark of an officer only in 1873. Ring collars were often beautifully handmade, chased and enameled works of jewelry. In the last years of the past century, the ring collar was reintroduced, serving only as an identifying mark of flag-bearers, staff sentries and staff orderlies of field police, but also as a medal for honoring regiments on appropriate historical anniversaries, such as the Prussian Grenadier Regiment No. 5 for the drummer, or the Prussian Garde du Corps Regiment, Life Guard Cuirassiers and Queen's Cuirassiers.

The chest armor of the heavy cavalry, the cuirassiers, more or less a relic of the knightly age, was especially eye-catching. Although the cuirass was no longer used in the field in Prussia after 1888, it was still worn in parades until 1914. In 1897 Kaiser Wilhelm II gave the Gardes du Corps Regiment a new outfit with a black cuirass, since their uniforms presented by the Tsar in 1814 were not only rather worn by that time but also no longer in harmony with the tastes of the time, on account of their dull form. Other German states had long since given up the cuirass, Saxony as early as 1825, Bavaria in 1873. It must be noted that French cuirassiers still rode into battle in 1914 with cuirasses (covered in field gray).

Many other details of equipment can be mentioned, such as the various belt buckles, bullet pouches, bandoliers and saber attachments, which can be seen clearly in original photos. Field belts and officers' belts show the state colors, the belt buckles bear the names or arms of the rulers. Various sleeve patches identify flag-bearers, semaphore signalmen, flagsmiths or men detailed for service, and sleeve stripes appear, such as the Gibraltar ribbon of the Hannover regiments. Shoulder cords and sleeve emblems for imperial and royal marksmanship prizes decorate the soldiers. Every detail of their equipment has its particular ornament, whether it be the straps and "Fröschel" of officers' saber attachments, the drum hooks of the musicians or the banner emblems of the buglers.

The cavalry took on a particular glamour with its parade blankets, caparisons and saddle cloths, plus harness set with shells or otherwise ornamented. The staff officers of the foot troops were also mounted and had decorated parade cloths, usually with the names of their ruling prince or bright emblems of orders.

Many other particulars brighten the picture of the Old Army. Even in the days of the Reichswehr (1919-1935) or the Wehrmacht of the Third Reich, there was still a whole series of uniform particulars and exceptions, of which nothing remains in the present day. Perhaps more thought will be given to tradition in the present Bundeswehr—a beginning of sorts has been made in the awarding of flags or the carrying of old emblems, such as the old Prussian guard star by the Feldjäger.

The white-red-yellow-light blue color scheme introduced in Prussia in 1816, with which at first the sword-knots of companies or squadrons were marked, and later the shoulder flaps of regiments and whole army corps, took on a particular importance. As the army was enlarged more and more, a fifth color, green, was added. This color sequence retained its meaning until the most recent past, and certain parallels still exist in the service-arm colors used today.

Württemberg: Flag-bearer's ring collar, M/1898.

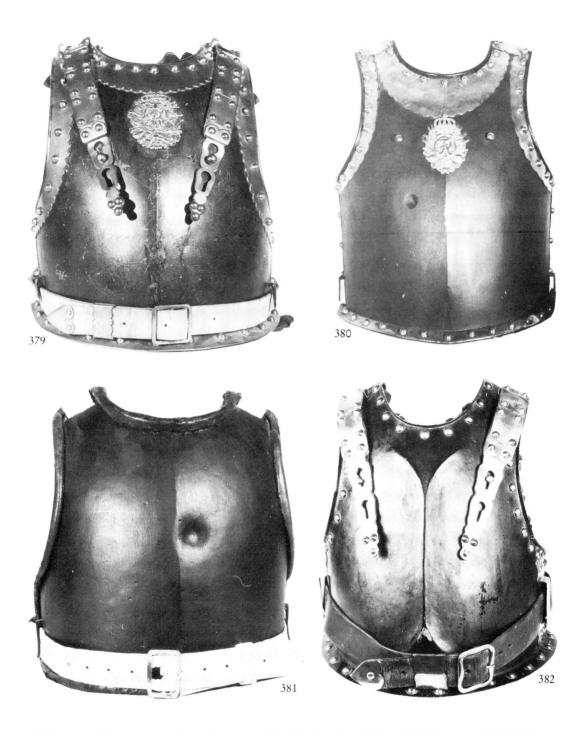

379

380

381

382

379 Prussia: Officer's cuirass from the reign of the "Soldier King" Friedrich Wilhelm I (1713-1740), with original cross-belting, the clasps with brass plates. Blackened iron, the edges covered with brass.

380 Prussia: Officer's cuirass from the reign of Frederick the Great (1740-1786).

381 Prussia: Enlisted men's cuirass from the same era (1740-1786), with original cross-belting (whitened tanned leather).

382 German Empire: Cuirass for officers of the Franconian area regiments, circa 1750, with original cross-belting.

383 Prussia: Black cuirass of the Gardes du Corps Regiment, presented by the Tsar of Russia in 1814 and worn only in parades; otherwise a yellow cuirass was worn. The chains were blackened, the edgings made of red wool.

384 Prussia: Black cuirass for officers of the Gardes du Corps Regiment, with the emblem on the chest, granted in 1912. In 1897 Kaiser Wilhelm II gave the regiment new, more elegant black cuirasses to mark the 100th birthday of his grandfather, Kaiser Wilhelm I.

385 Prussia: Cuirass for enlisted men of the Queen's Cuirassier Regiment (Pomeranian) No. 2, of Pasewalk, with the chest emblem granted in 1895 (screwed-on ring collar). The Life Guard Cuirassier Regiment "Great Elector" (Silesian) No. 1 likewise wore the ring collar attached to the cuirass.

386 Prussia: Officer's cuirass of the line regiments, nickel-plated with gold borders; elegant style used post-1900.

In the court and bodyguard troops of the various dynasties we find the origins of standing armies; at least most of the guard and elite regiments trace their histories back to such troop units formed in early days.

The oldest documentable troop unit in the German Army is the Royal Bavarian Life Guard Halberdiers, mentioned in a document as early as 1580, with its origins probably traceable to duty at the Residence in Munich. In 1580 the Halberdiers' uniform was described as "black wool trimmed with velvet . . . equipped with long sleeves and coattails", from which one can gather that the old-fashioned uniforms worn until 1852, with Casaque and hat, still largely represented the uniforms of the 16th Century. In 1852 the Halberdiers received a new uniform with a silver-trimmed service jacket and a German silver helmet with white hair plume, with a standing lion for full-dress occasions. In 1919, after the collapse of the old monarchies, this oldest German guard unit was disbanded.

Unfortunately, there are practically no remaining written descriptions or uniform regulations for this oldest guard unit (not even about the new uniforms of 1852), since the files in question were sacrificed to a scrap paper drive (de facto thrift) in the 19th Century.

Here it is appropriate to note the undeniable relationship between the Bavarian Halberdiers and the Austrian Archer Life Guards: both terms originated linguistically in the medieval word "arciarius": bowman (from the Latin "arcus": bow. In the Midele Ages, bowmen were already the bodyguards of royalty. In France and England they were "archers", in Italy "acieri." In terms of uniforms too, Bavarian halberdiers and Austrian archers show great similarities; until 1850 their uniforms were stylistically the same, and the Bavarian troops followed the style of the Austrian helmets and uniforms from 1852 on.

In the Kingdom of Prussia, King Friedrich II established a mounted life guard unit in 1740, under the name "Garde du Corps", a troop that became the favorite regiment of the last German Emperor and King of Prussia, Wilhelm II (1888-1918) The full-dress uniforms of the Garde du Corps, with a red outer vest and embroidered guard star, was retained until the monarchy ended. In addition to the Garde du Corps, King Friedrich Wilhelm IV founded a Sergeants' Guard Company in 1829; as of 1861 it was called the Castle Guard Company. Its assignment was the guarding of the royal castles and gardens; it was given a particularly splendid traditional uniform that is shown on the following pages. In 1866, after the annexation of Electoral Hesse, the Life Guard from there was absorbed (and placed on a basis of attrition as of 1867, with no new replacements taken). A newer mounted court troop unit was the Prussian Life Guard Gendarmes, founded in 1820 and divided into two platoons in 1889, following the Russian model (the 1st Platoon was the Life Guards of His Majesty the Emperor and King, the 2nd the Life Guards of Her Majesty the Empress and Queen). Here too, the full-dress uniforms used followed the pattern set by Frederick the Great, representing Kaiser Wilhelm II's fondness for his ancestors.

The Royal Württemberg Castle Guard Company cannot look back so directly to an old establishment date, as the territories of the "Swabian District" were too divided, and only in 1806, with the establishment of the Kingdom of Württemberg, did a remarkable military unity come about in the young kingdom. The Mounted Life Guards were established in 1809—and wore a picturesque iron bow helmet with a mighty crest—but by 1816 they had been turned into a regular regiment. The founding day of the Württemberg Castle Guard Company was July 9, 1872, making it the youngest guard unit in the German Army; the core of the company were members of the disbanded Feldjäger Squadron, an earlier troop resembling the police.

The Kingdom of Saxony had no guard unit as well defined as those of the other kingdoms; the 1st (Life Guard) Grenadier Regiment No. 100 and the Cavalry Guard Regiment provided the necessary guard and sentry services at official occasions. The Life Guard Grenadier Regiment was established in 1670 as a guard unit; in 1806, when the Kingdom of Saxony was established, it was first called the "King's Regiment", then in 1813 the "Provisional Guard Regiment"—the name cited above was used as of 1867.

The uniform of the Life Guard Grenadier Regiment basically corresponds to that of the infantry guards in Prussia and Germany as a whole, having no special parade uniforms or helmets. The Cavalry Guard Regiment, on the other hand, received in 1907, along with its usual normal cuirassier-type uniforms, the silver springing lion for its helmets, to be worn in parades instead of the helmet spike. The Cavalry Guard Regiment originated in the "German Mounted Life Guards" of 1680, renamed the "King's Cuirassiers" in 1806 and given their final name in 1822 and/or 1876.

The following court troops existed in the smaller states:

The Kingdom of Hannover, which existed until 1866, had no unit functioning solely as a guard or court troop; the guard regiment (Infantry Guards) and Cavalry Guard, and in particular the imposingly uniformed Gardes du Corps Regiment, performed the necessary guard duties.

In the Grand Duchy of Hesse-Darmstadt the Mounted Life Guards existed since 1623; later they were renamed the Sergeants' Guard Company, and they were not mounted after 1849. Their uniforms generally corresponded to those of other German infantry guards, including a leather helmet with silvered trim.

The Grand Duchy of Mecklenburg-Schwerin had a Mounted Life Guard as of 1782, but it was disbanded in 1803. In 1810 the members of the former Life Guard were absorbed into the 3rd Company of the Grenadier Guard Battalion. After numerous changes, Mecklenburg-Schwerin joined the III. Prussian Army Corps in 1849. Since 1867 the 1st Battalion of Grenadier Regiment No. 89 performed guard duties and wore a bearskin cap of Napoleonic pattern in addition to their regular uniforms for the occasion.

Saxony: Officer's cartridge case of the Cavalry Guards, post-1879.

419

420

421

419 Prussia: The Castle Guard Company in the White Hall of the Berlin Castle on New Year's Day, 1913. At the far left is Captain Pfanneberg in the uniform of the Commander.

420 Bavaria: Sub-Brigadier (comparable to a lieutenant) of the Royal Bavarian Life Guard Halberdiers in full-dress uniform with coat. Picture taken in 1905.

421 Bavaria: Sub-Brigadier of the Halberdiers in service uniform, picture taken in 1905.

Worrld War I had been going on for more than four years when, on November 3, 1918, the seamen in Kiel mutinied and the revolution quickly broke out in all the larger German cities. The first to abdicate was the King of Bavaria, Ludwig III, on November 7, 1918. In Prussia, Imperial Chancellor Max von Baden unilaterally announced the abdication of Kaiser and King Wilhelm II, Friedrich Ebert became Chancellor, and Scheidemann proclaimed the Republic in the Reichstag. In the morning hours of November 10, 1918, Kaiser Wilhelm II left his headquarters at Spa by railroad; for reasons of security, he crossed the border into Holland by car, and then awaited the following express train at the depot of Eijsden, Holland. The government of The Netherlands was very surprised, and finally offered Amerongen Castle of Count Bentinck as his first place of exile. Their Wilhelm II lived for more than a year with his consort, Empress Auguste Viktoria, who had come to join him, as guests of the Count. In 1920 Wilhelm II obtained Huis Doorn in the Province of Utrecht, and on May 15, 1920 he moved into the renovated little castle. Empress Auguste Viktoria died at Doorn on April 11, 1921, and shortly thereafter the Kaiser married Hermine von Schönaich-Carolath, born a Princess of Reuss. Wilhelm II died at Doorn on June 4, 1941, at the age of eighty-two (he was born January 27, 1859).

Through an agreement with the State of Prussia, Wilhelm II was allowed to take a large number of pieces of furniture and art treasures from his castles in Prussia to Doorn. Although he had abdicated, he still regarded himself as Emperor and King, and even while in exile, he always wore a uniform to appropriate events. For this purpose, taking into account his figure, which had changed with age, he had a great number of uniforms tailored, which were made to the usual quality according to the regulations for the "Future Peacetime Uniform" of 1915.

Wilhelm II was Chief and Incumbent of numerous German and foreign regiments, as well as a Prussian and Bavarian Field Marshal; foreign ranks of Field Marshal were also accorded him, as shown on the facsimile of the 1914 Service Rank List.

As Commander-in-Chief, Wilhelm II also had the right to wear any other German uniform, which he did with the uniforms of regiments to which, for various reasons, he felt particularly close; thus he wore the uniforms of the Tsar Alexander Grenadier Guard Regiment No. 1, the Kaiser Franz Grenadier Guard Regiment No. 2 or the 1st Dragoon Guard Regiment, whose Chief was his grandmother, Queen Victoria of Great Britain. At Huis Doorn, not only the furnishings of the house have been largely preserved, but the Kaiser's collection of uniforms and equipment has been preserved to a great degree too, and is well preserved and protected. Doorn Castle is now owned by the government of The Netherlands and can be visited during the summer months as the museum of the "Huis Doorn Foundation." At this time, great portions of the Kaiser's helmets, uniforms, weapons and medals can be seen in a special display. Selections from this rich collection are shown on the following pages.

Chief of the Army
His Majesty the Emperor and King
Wilhelm
His Majesty the Kaiser's and King's
Regiments:
Royal Prussian 1st Foot Guard Regiment, Chief 6/15/1888; Grenadier Regiment King Friedrich Wilhelm I (2nd East Prussian) No. 3, Chief 9/9/1901; Grand Ducal Mecklenburg Fusilier Regiment No. 90 "Kaiser Wilhelm", Chief 8/26/1911; 2nd Baden Grenadier Regiment "Kaiser Wilhelm I" No. 110, Chief 9/13/1893; Kaiser Wilhelm Infantry Regiment (2nd Grand Ducal Hessian) No. 116, Chief 9/12/1891; King's Infantry Regiment No. 145, Chief 9/4/1893; Regiment of the Gardes du Corps, Chief 6/15/1888; Life Guard Hussar Regiment, Chief 6/19/1888; King's Uhlan Regiment (1st Hannover) No. 13, Chief 9.13.1889; King's Mounted Jäger Regiment No. 1, Chief 8.8.1905; 1st Field Artillery Guard Regiment, Chief 9/1/1888.
Life Guard Regiments: Grenadier Life Guard Regiment "King Friedrich Wilhelm III (1st Brandenburg) No. 8, Cuirassier Life Guard Regiment "Great Elector" (Silesian) No. 1, 1st Hussar Life Guard Regiment No. 1; 2nd Hussar Life Guard Regiment "Queen Victoria of Prussia" No. 2.
Royal Bavarian 6th Infantry Regiment "Kaiser Wilhelm, King of Prussia", Incumbent 1/25/1896; 1st Uhlan Regiment "Kaiser Wilhelm II, King of Prussia", Incumbent 6/19/1888
Royal Saxon 2nd Grenadier Regiment No. 101 "Kaiser Wilhelm, King of Prussia", Chief 4/9/1999; 3rd Uhlan Regiment No. 21 "Kaiser Wilhelm, King of Prussia", Chief 10/25/1905.

Chef der Armee
Seine Majestät der Kaiser und König
⚜ Wilhelm. ⚜
Seiner Majestät des Kaisers und Königs
Regimenter ꝛc.

Kgl. Preuß. 1. Garde-R. z. F., Chef 15. 6. 88; Gren.-R. König Friedrich Wilhelm I. (2. Ostpreuß.) Nr. 3, Chef 9. 9. 01; Großherzogl. Mecklenb. Füs. R. Nr. 90 Kaiser Wilhelm, Chef 26. 8. 11; 2. Bad. Gren.-R. Kaiser Wilhelm I. Nr. 110, Chef 13. 9. 93; Inf.-R. Kaiser Wilhelm (2. Großherzogl. Hess.) Nr. 116, Chef 12. 9. 91; Königs-Inf.-R. Nr. 145, Chef 4. 9. 93. R. der Gardes du Corps, Chef 15. 6. 88; Leib-Garde-Hus.-R., Chef 19. 6. 88; Königs-Ulan.-R. (1. Hannov.) Nr. 13, Chef 13. 9. 89; R. Königs-Jäg.z.Pf. Nr. 1, Chef 8. 8. 05; 1. Garde-Feldart.-R., Chef 1. 9. 88.

Leib-Regtr.: Leib-Gren.-R. König Friedrich Wilhelm III. (1. Brandenb.) Nr. 8. Leib-Kür.-R. Großer Kurfürst (Schles.) Nr. 1. 1. Leib-Hus.-R. Nr. 1. 2. Leib-Hus.-R. Königin Victoria v. Preußen Nr. 2.

Kgl. Bayer. 6. Inf.-R. Kaiser Wilhelm, König v. Preußen. Inh. 25. 1. 96; 1. Ulan.-R. Kaiser Wilhelm II., König v. Preußen. Inh. 19. 6. 88.

Kgl. Sächs. 2. Gren.-R. Nr. 101. „Kaiser Wilhelm, König v. Preußen", Chef 9. 4. 88. 3. Ulan.-R. Nr. 21 „Kaiser Wilhelm, König von Preußen", Chef 25. 10. 05.

Kgl. Württ. Inf.-R. Kaiser Wilhelm, König v. Preußen (2. Württ.) Nr. 120, Chef 22. 6. 88. Drag.-R. Königin Olga (1. Württ.) Nr. 25, Chef 7. 9. 09.

Feldmarschall des Kais. u. Kgl. Öster. u. Ungar. Heeres 4. 5. 00. Kais. u. Kgl. Öster. Inf.-R. Wilhelm I, Deutscher Kaiser u. König von Preußen Nr. 34. Oberst-Inh. 16. 6. 88; Hus.-R. Wilhelm II., Deutscher Kaiser u. König v. Preußen Nr. 7. Oberst-Inh. 18. 9. 85.

Kais. Russ. Leib-Garde St. Petersburger R. König Friedrich Wilhelm III., Chef 18. 6. 88; 85. Inf. Wyborg Sr. Kais. u. Kgl. Maj. Kaiser v. Deutschland, König v. Preußen Wilhelm II. R., Chef 18. 5. 84; Hus.-R. Narwa Nr. 13, Chef 12. 9. 01. (Leibgarde-Hus.-R. Grodno. 7. 11. 10.) Admiral d. Kais. Russischen Flotte. 7. 8. 97.

Feldmarschall d. Kgl. Großbrit. Heeres 27. 1. 01. Kgl. Großbrit. 1. (Royal) Dragoons-R., Chef 5. 5. 94. Admiral of the fleet der Kgl. Großbrit. Marine. 2. 8. 89.

Admiral der Kgl. Schwed. Marine. 30. 8. 88.

Admiral der Kgl. Norweg. Marine. 1890.

Admiral der Kgl. Dänisch. Marine. 2. 4. 03.

Ehren-Generalkapitän der Kgl. Spanisch. Armee. 22. 12. 04. Kgl. Spanisch. Drag.-R. Numancia Nr. 11., Ehren-Oberst 22. 12. 04.

Ehren-Admiral d. Kgl. Griechisch. Marine. 12. 4. 05.

Royal Württemberg Infantry Regiment "Kaiser Wilhelm, King of Prussia" (2nd Württemberg) No. 120, Chief 6/22/1888; Dragoon Regiment "Queen Olga" (1st Württemberg) No. 25, Chief 9/7/1909.

Field Marshal of the Imperial and Royal Austrian and Hungarian Army 5/4/1900. Imperial and Royal Austrian Infantry Regiment "Wilhelm I, German Emperor and King of Prussia" No. 34, Colonel-Incumbent 6/16/1888; Hussar Regiment "Wilhelm II, German Emperor and King of Prussia" No. 7, Colonel-Incumbent 9/19/1885.

Imperial Russian Life Guard St. Petersburg Regiment "King Friedrich Wilhelm III", Chief 6/18/1888; 85th Infantry Wyborg "His Imperial and Royal Majesty Emperor of Germany, King of Prussia Wilhelm II" Regiment, Chief 5/18/1884; Hussar Regiment Narwa No. 13; Chief 9/12/1901; (Life Guard Hussar Regiment Grodno 11/7/1910), Admiral of the Imperial Russian Fleet 8/7/1897.

Field Marshal of the Royal British Army 1/27/1901; Royal British 1st (Royal) Dragoon Regiment, Chief 5/5/1894; Admiral of the Fleet of the Royal British Navy 8/2/1889.

Admiral of the Royal Swedish Navy 8/30/1888.

Admiral of the Royal Norwegian Navy, 1890.

Admiral of the Royal Danish Navy, 4/2/1903.

Honorary Captain-General of the Royal Spanish Army, 12/22/1904; Royal Spanish Dragoon Regiment Numancia No. 11, Honorary Colonel 12/22/1904.

Honorary Admiral of the Royal Greek Navy, 4/12/1905.

Though the soldier's position was little respected in the 18th Century, and even regarded as a burdensome, often life-threatening oppression, during the Wars of Liberation the popular spirit identified with the German rulers' desire to free themselves from Napoleon's rule, and this new national enthusiasm, arising almost on impulse, led to the formation of numerous volunteer units. Naturally this national enthusiasm, which is known to us today only in the form of written documents, was guided by the aristocracy; the simple peasant woman or the widow living alone in the city had little or no understanding of such things if her breadwinner had gone off to war or fallen in battle. Thus the enthusiastic reports of the commanders and the poets surely contradict the reality of the matter, and the enthusiasm itself may well have ended with the slightest wound, for there was as good as no medical, let alone medicinal, treatment of wounded men. Field surgeons were very much the exception. Still in all, one can assume that at least at that time the soldier's position gained a good deal of respect, which continued to grow in the long peacetime years of the Biedermeier era, though there were no more important battles then. The revolutions of 1848, the regional wars of 1864 and 1866, did not demand any particularly great sacrifices. Even the war of 1870-71, supported by great national pride and leading to the proclamation of the second German Empire, could awaken only positive feelings in the people. Thus at the end of the past century the soldier, whether officer or man, was looked upon with pride.

A great number of mementos became documents of this duty that was military service. For the ranks, reservist pictures were created in lithograph or oil, often with a photograph of the man glued on, and depending on how much art one could afford, the pictures were set in expensive hand-carved frames or bought readymade. There were also reservist beer mugs of porcelain or stoneware, reservist beer glasses, pitchers, liquor bottles, plates, platters, bowls, egg-cups, chamberpots and many other utensils of daily life that were equipped with colorful scenes of army life, plus the soldier's name and dates of service. Military utensils like epaulettes, 'Sabre-Tache's', or artillery shells were made into reservist mementos. The number of souvenirs of military service made of bone, carved wood, lamps, plaques or beer pendants for watch-chains is incalculable. Well-to-do soldiers could afford expensive photo albums. In the country or the provinces there were pictures of saints and votive tablets with military themes, especially when a soldier was killed or severely injured and invalided in carrying out his military duty. In World War I, the industry went overboard producing low-priced picture frames of wood or metal in the shape of the Iron Cross, especially for the purpose of giving photos of fallen soldiers.

Retirement gifts for officers, especially those of the nobility, naturally differ basically from the reservist souvenirs of the common soldier. Statuettes of bronze or silver, usually portraying uniformed figures from the glorious regiments of the 18th Century or the Wars of Liberation, were especially popular, as were figures portraying the rulers of the German states. Silver helmets as drinking cups, life-size or miniature, became favorite souvenirs of the guard regiments in particular. Desk plaques, oil paintings, silver bottle openers, drinking cups, cigar clippers and table utensils were more or less common.

The medium of photography gave the officer class the possibility of presenting an album to a deserving commander of member of the officers' corps on a service anniversary or at retirement, in which all the members of the officers' corps were represented by photographs. The covers of such albums were appropriately lavishly decorated, depending on the regiment and the occasion.

The classic gift to honor the officer was naturally the saber, which was presented in costly form, with exquisite fittings and high-quality Damascus blade.

The higher the rank and position of the recipient, the more lavish and expensive these gifts became, often taking on the proportions of miniature monuments.

For centuries, officers' portraits have been a part of the ancestral galleries in castles and manors. The numerous portraits of officers, frequently found in private ownership, have provided important information to the study of uniforms, especially because many preserved uniform specifications have been corrected or at least varied thanks to such pictures. Naturally it was only the financially more prosperous officers, whether noble or bourgeois, who could afford to have their portraits painted in uniform. The invention of photography allowed everyone to leave a picture of himself for posterity. In the days before World War I, there was as yet no color photography, and the black-and-white photographs were often colored by hand, which naturally led to falsification of the originals, whether by unnatural or inaccurate colors, changes in perspective or simply faulty work. Very often the pictures were retouched to make them look better or suit the vanity of the photographed man, as has often happened to photographs of highly placed people.

Prussia:
A Hussar in an artist's studio, "riding" model. Picture taken circa 1895.

"Like father, like son," one could say of children's uniforms. For the son was naturally proud of his soldier father, and the proud father in turn tried as soon as possible—through play—to awaken his son's enthusiasm at being a soldier. The military tradition was dominant in officers' families; it was found more rarely among non-commissioned officers and was definitely the exception among the ranks. Children's uniforms, usually worn by boys from four to eight years old, naturally showed the father's exact rank and position and, depending on the father's financial means, these uniforms were as precise and of as high quality as he could afford. Thus there were "store-bought" uniforms as well as individual ones made by a tailor or uniform supplier, the latter representing the father's uniform to the smallest detail.

Besides these specially prepared types, there were also products purely for play, that could be bought just as one can buy a cowboy or Indian costumes from a department store or mail-order house today. The preparation of these play uniforms was naturally simple: helmets were made of thin sheet metal or cardboard, uniforms generally of thin felt or consisting only of a paper jacket representing an Ulanka or a Hussar's Atilla. Naturally these toys were not especially durable, especially when used in "heavy combat." The sabers or swords imitated the World War I models, such as the M/1852 or M/1889 cavalry sabers, the M/1889 infantry officer's sword or the Cuirassier's Pallasch, sometimes cheaply made of thin sheet metal, sometimes accurate models with heavy cast and chased hilts and Damascus blades just like the real officer's swords. One remaining original piece even bears the etched name of the boy and the slogan, "A long life to the regiment that proudly calls itself 'The Wild Ones'."

All the accompanying pieces of equipment also existed as exact models, such as epaulettes, shoulder pieces, belts, sword-belts, cartridge cases, saber sheaths, caparisons and harness for the hobbyhorse, rifles and pistols. Drums, bugles, kettledrums, fifes and flutes were naturally also available.

These items—though they applied in terms of uniforms to the Imperial past—were manufactured and sold even during World War II, as old mail-order catalogs show. As a toy, the Wehrmacht uniform obviously had little chance of selling, and the parents' conservative outlook determined what the manufacturers made.

The situation was very different as concerned the uniforms of princes of ruling houses. Since olden times it was the custom that the Prussian princes entered the 1st Foot Guard Regiment at the age of ten. Similar practices existed in the other German kingdoms and principalities, where great emphasis was placed on the military education of sons. The uniforms and equipment made for them had nothing to do with toys; they were exact models of prescribed uniforms scaled down to fit the young princes.

447

448

449

447 Bavaria: Crown Prince Rupprecht (1869-1955) and his son Luitpold (1901-1914) inspect the 1st Field Artillery Regiment "Prince Regent Luitpold." Hereditary Prince Luitpold became a lieutenant in the 1st Field Artillery Regiment on March 12, 1912, the 91st birthday of his great-grandfather Prince Regent Luitpold. The little prince died of polio on August 27, 1914.

448 Saxony: A proud first lieutenant of the field artillery reserve with his son, who wears the uniform of the Royal Saxon Cadets. Picture taken circa 1915.

449 Prussia: A lieutenant general in uniform, with his family. Of his eight sons, seven entered the army. From left to right: Field Artillery Regiment, Ordnance Inspector-General, (2nd Brandenburg) No. 18; civilian; 1st Foot Guard Regiment, Sergeant of Dragoons; the mother; the father; Grenadier Regiment "King Friedrich Wilhelm IV" (1st Pomeranian) No. 2; Kaiser Franz Grenadier Guard Regiment No. 2; 1st Field Artillery Guard Regiment; and Cadet of the Chief Cadet Training School, Berlin-Lichterfelde.

_450_ A little Bavarian field artilleryman practices saluting—picture taken circa 1910.

_451_ This little Uhlan in a sailor suit was photographed in Frankfurt-am-Main in 1862.

_452_ Members of ruling houses naturally set a good example in military matters too: Prince Friedrich of Prussia, born in 1911 and photographed in the autumn of 1915, uniformed as a field-gray "Lieutenant of the Guard", gazes proudly from his easy chair.

_453_ A field-gray "Lieutenant of the Infantry", wearing a substantially accurate M/1910 uniform, sent this picture to his aunt for Christmas in the war year of 1914.

456
457
458
459

456 Bavaria: Child's uniform of 1910, patterned after a first lieutenant's uniform of the 2nd Bavarian Uhlan Regiment of Ansbach.

457 Bavaria: Child's uniform, circa 1914, patterned after a sergeant's uniform of the 2nd Light Horse Regiment "Taxis" of Regensburg.

458 Prussia: Child's uniform, circa 1910, patterned after a cuirassier's uniform of the Count Wrangel Cuirassier Regiment (East Prussian) No. 3.

459 German Empire: Cilnd's cuirass and helmet, circa 1910, patterned on the equipment of a Pappenheim Cuirassier of the Thirty Years' War.

460

460 German Empier: Group of children's uniforms, circa 1910: Infantry first lieutenant's jacket with helmet, Bavarian cuirass, Prussian cuirassier's helmet, saber, and cartridge case of the Hussar Life Guards of Potsdam, drum, belt, epaulettes, cap and various sabers.

461 Mecklenburg-Schwerin: Child's "Infantry" helmet of pressed cardboard, circa 1900.

462 Württemberg: Uhlan's chapka for a child, with field-gray trim, made of lacquered cardboard, circa 1915.

463 Prussia: Child's helmet for "Cuirassier Guards", circa 1910.

464 Bavaria: Overcoat of a child's uniform of the 2nd Light Horse Regiment, circa 1912.

465 Prussia: Fur cap of the "Hussar Life Guards", of cardboard and black plush, with paper guard star, circa 1900.

466 Prussia: Child's "Garde du Corps" helmet, sheet metal with wooden eagle, circa 1900.

Information on militaria collections of the 9th Century is—compared to that on weapon collections—scarcely in existence. Only toward the end of the century were there a number of private collectors whose collections were ultimately documented in the form of auction catalogs. Collectors' listings were probably not made, as none exist. Reference works as we know them today did not exist either, apart from the often lavishly illustrated uniform books, but in general there were no precise details as to when various pieces of uniforms and equipment were introduced. Only the work of Krickel/Lange, *The German Empire's Army*, published in Berlin in 1892, began to portray details of equipment, though still without exact data. Professor Richard Knötel began his large-scale *Uniform Data* in 1896, Karl Müller and Louis Braun published their standard work on the Royal Bavarian Army in installments beginning in 1906, and Paul Pietsch wrote on Prussian uniforms in 1912, offering a sort of continuation of C. Kling's book, published in the same year, on Prussia up to 1806. Paul Pietsch lived to enjoy the rare pleasure of seeing his book on uniforms published in expanded form more than fifty years later. Beyond this, the military collector had to make do as best he could for a long time, by studying uniform regulations, seeking bits of information on uniforms in regimental histories, and often talking with old soldiers to obtain information.

The best-known private collections of the era around 1900 were:

The collection of battle-scene painter Prof. Louis Braun (1836-1916), displayed in Munich and in his Wernfels Castle near Nürnberg. Braun began his collection with the 16th Century and specialized in the era from 1800 to 1871. The collection was auctioned off in Munich in 1914, during Louis Braun's lifetime, and an illustrated catalog exists.

A Mr. Bartsch (more exact information is lacking) owned an extensive collection that emphasized the Battle of Nations at Leipzig; it was kept in a building near the battle monument, and a thorough catalog is supposed to have existed. In World War II the greater part of the collection was lost; only a small part of it was saved and is now in the Leipzig Museum of City History.

A Mr. Buhrig of Leipzig also owned an extensive collection of militaria from the Wars of Liberation. This collection was auctioned in Leipzig in 1913; an illustrated catalog still exists.

Major F. W. Deiss, who died in Darmstadt in 1931 (author of the well-known work *The German Soldier's Book*), owned an excellent collection, particularly of Hessian militaria, which was placed in the Darmstadt Castle Museum around 1924.

The church official Franz Bonsack of Apfelstädt, near Arnstadt in the Gotha district, owned what was probably the most extensive collection of militaria that was ever in private hands. He began to collect in 1891, as a small boy, and was able to put his collection on public display at Friedenstein Castle in Gotha as of 1930. Over 400 complete uniforms, more than 1000 helmets and an incalculable quantity of effects, equipment, pictures and documents, cuirasses, swords and guns were displayed. In addition, Bonsack also displayed part of his collection at Wachsenburg Castle near Gotha. There are contradictory reports of the fate of his collection after 1945. A large portion of it was taken to the Berlin Armory, while other portions were lent out and are now in the possession of state museums in East Germany. Parts of the collection were probably lost.

Carl Hollitzer, historical painter, lived in Deutsch-Altenburg on the Danube from 1874 to 1942. Along with an extensive collection of costumes, he owned one of the best military collections, with its emphasis on the Wars of Liberation. Hollitzer bought, among others, many parts of the collections of Louis Braun, Robert von Haug, Sigismund L'Allemand, Baron von Myrbach, Rudolf von Ottenfeld and Professor C. Seiler. Hollitzer had his entire collection auctioned at the Vienna Dorotheum during his lifetime (1934), but sadly learned that interest in his treasures was very limited and a large portion remained unsold—which he gladly retained.

Professor Robert von Haug, military and equine painter (1857-1922), lived in Stuttgart. There are no documents on his collection. But since they were acquired by Hollitzer in Vienna, they must have emphasized pieces from the Napoleonic era.

Anton Hoffmann, historical painter from Munich (1863-1938), owned a splendid collection of almost exclusively Bavarian militaria, which was inherited by his housekeeper after his death and gradually sold off to costume houses and junk shops.

Angelo Jank, Bavarian military and equine painter, lived in Munich from 1868 to 1940. He also owned a predominantly Bavarian but also French-oriented collection, the best pieces of which went to the Bavarian Army Museum.

Professor Sigismund L'Allemand of Vienna owned a large collection of militaria, which was likewise purchased by Hollitzer.

Ferdinand Theodor Muhsfeldt, who died in Hamburg in 1924, was a well-known collector of military lore, whose militaria collection was sold in 1937 via a fixed-price catalog. Thus numbers of pieces have been preserved: there were 109 helmets, over 150 swords, 90 rifles, carbines and pistols, and over 70 cuirasses, as well as epaulettes. saber sheaths. ring collars etc.

Felician, Baron von Myrbach, historical painter, was born in 1863, lived in Paris and Vienna, and owned an interesting study collection of militaria, which was purchased by Hollitzer in Vienna.

Rudolf von Ottenfeld, 1856-1913, military painter and co-author with Professor Oskar Teuber of a well-known book on the Austrian Army, which was published in Vienna in 1895, owned an extensive, mainly Austrian-oriented collection, which was also purchased by Hollitzer.

Prince Karl of Prussia (1801-1883), the brother of Kaiser Wilhelm I, assembled an extensive collection of weapons and militaria, part of which was displayed in Glienicke Castle near Potsdam. After the Prince died, the collection was placed in the Berlin Hall of Fame (Armory), where it formed an extensive foundation for the subsequently famous Armory collection.

Friedrich Rascher, painter, lived in Frankfurt and died around 1930, and was a zealous collector of weapons, helmets and uniforms. He was so wrapped up in militaria that, at the worst time, in 1919, he founded a journal for collectors of militaria (*Archives for Weapon and Uniform Data, 1919-1921*), which got him into great financial difficulties. Some of his finest helmets were documented in his journal. Rascher originally lent his collection to the Darmstadt Castle Museum, where it ultimately remained.

Professor C. Sailer lived in Munich; exact dates are unknown. He owned an extensive collection of costumes and uniforms, which was auctioned in Munich in 1921.

At the Wachsenburg near Gotha, a collection of uniforms was set up as early as 1911, based on an impressive collection of militaria emphasizing the 1813-1871 era. This collection belonged to three men from Eisenach, and the sum of 22,000 gold marks was collected from the German Princes and the War Ministry to buy the collection for the Wachsenburg display in 1909.

There must have been other good old collections, but—as mentioned at the start—there are scarcely any reports of them.

Goermneltal collections of uniforms and equipment existed in Berlin, Munich, Dresden and Stuttgart.

The Berlin Armory (Zeughaus) was opened as a military museum in 1880—after an appropriate earlier history—and its collection became the largest in Germany. The Army Museum in Munich was founded in 1879 and obtained its own building at the Court Gardens in Munich in 1905. The Army Museum in Dresden originated in the old weapon collection od the 15th-Century Saxon dukes; it was opened to the public in 1876 as a new, independent collection including French weapons captured in 1870-71. The extensive collections were already documented by catalogs before World War I. During World War II the museum buildings were destroyed; the contents had generally been taken to safety and still exist, though decimated by plundering and lack of care. The Stuttgart Army Museum was housed in the Old Castle until 1931 and was burned out in that year. In 1932 another army museum was opened, this one in the New Castle. The contents were lost during and after World War II.

Among those founded between the two World Wars are the Baden Army Museum in Karlsruhe, the Navy Museum in Berlin, and the Army and Weapon Historical Department of the State Museum of Danzig History in Danzig-Oliva. An extensive collection of uniforms and weapons was established in the former Residence Castle of Darmstadt in 1923, comprising not only the gigantic private collection of the last Grand Duke of Hesse-Darmstadt, Ernst Ludwig (founded by Landgrave Ludwig IX circa 1780) and the following components: Mementos owned by the former Grand Ducal Hessian regiments, such as silver items and paintings; the collections of F. Rascher and Major Deiss; items from the State Museum's collection of weapons and uniforms as well as the large collection of over 100 gun models from all over the world, which were provided by the Technical College of Darmstadt. The Darmstadt collection was lost in World War II, since the objects were not put in safekeeping. Thus bombs destroyed more than 100 complete uniforms plus the weapon, medal and military musical instrument collections, not to mention an extensive library. A small portion of these treasures could be saved and is again displayed at the Darmstadt Castle Museum today.

Large private collections were put on public display in 1935 at the Historic Military Museum of Koblenz and in 1938 at the Altenburg Regimental Museum. In many Wehrmacht garrisons, with the help of the officers' organizations of the Old Army, uniform collections were established, mainly covering the 1900-1918 era. All of these collections were lost in World War II.

Today two large state collections exist in the Federal Republic: The Museum of Military History in Rastatt, which was first established in Baden-Baden in 1949 as the "Baden Historical Museum—New Castle" and moved to its present domicile in Rastatt Castle in 1957; and the Bavarian Army Museum, the greater part of its collection having been saved and put on display at the ducal castle in Ingolstadt since 1969.

Today as well, various units of the Bundeswehr have set up display collections, often built up laboriously, piece by piece, to show present-day soldiers the history of the army and its uniforms. Many state, city and regional museums in the Federal Republic often display little-known items of uniform history, so that a trip to a museum, even in one's own area, can be worthwhile for the uniform enthusiast. Inquiries are often necessary in advance, but it is easy to inform oneself, what with the museum guides presently published.

In Schwarzburg (in East Germany) the "Schwarzburg Armory" collection was founded in the 15th Century and became a well-known princely collection before 1918. Among its possessions were the complete equipment of a Schwarzburg company of 1630, mementos of Gustav Adolf, and equipment of the Schwarzburg-Rudolstadt Army from all times. There were also costly uniforms presented by various German princes. In 1940 these items were stored in Heidecksburg Castle; they survived the last war and are displayed today in the State Museum of Heidecksburg-Rudolstadt, with a catalog available.

The Arsenal in East Berlin has come back to life in its impressive, splendidly constructed quarters as the Museum of German History, and its two catalogs in book form give a good overview of its headgear and swords.

The Army Museum of the GDR in Dresden also shows the interested visitor many components of old weapons and uniforms, from bygone days to modern times.

Prussia: Generals' uniforms, old and new models, 1909.

469

469 Former Armory, Berlin: Figurine with the uniform of a cuirassier of the von Bohlen Cuirassier Regiment No. 1, 1786. Picture taken circa 1938,

470 Prussia: Facsimile from the "Official Guide to the Royal Arsenal of Berlin", 1914.

471

471 Reprint from the illustrated guide to the Royal Bavarian Army Museum, L. Wacker Publishers, Munich-Pasing, 1912: Picture of Room VI, with uniforms and weapons from the time of Elector Karl Theodor (1777-1799), including Rumford casquettes and uniforms in the showcase.

472

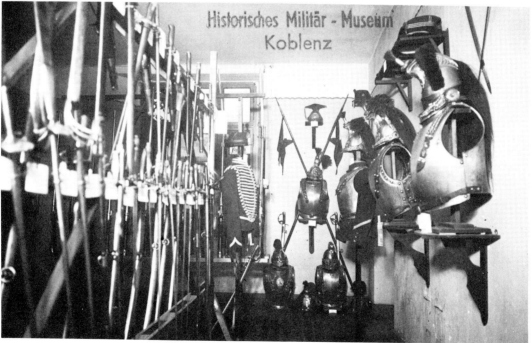

473

472-473 Original photos of portions of the collections in the Historical Military Museum of Koblenz, circa 1938.

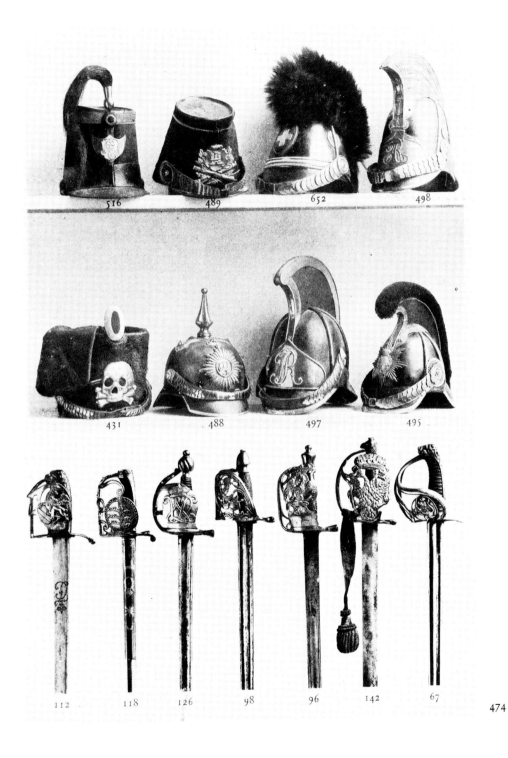

474 Bavaria: Reprint from the auction catalog *Collection of Prof. Louis Braun*, Helbing Gallery, Munich, 1914, showing Pallaches from the 18th and 19th Centuries and helmets (516: officer's shako from the city of Schwäbisch Hall, 1848; shako and helmet of the Hamburg Home Guard (189 & 488), Saxon cavalry helmets (495, 497, 498); fur cap M/1850 of the Prussian 1st Hussar Life Guard Regiment (431) and Swiss Light Cavalry officer's helmet (652).

533 534 532

481 482 509

512 508 540

475

475 Bavaria: Reprint from the catalog *Collection of Prof. Louis Brau*, with Austrian cuirassier officers'
helmets (532-534), a dragoon officer's helmet from Baden (481), Uhlan officer's chapka from Baden,
circa 1813 (482), Uhlan guard officer's shako from Württemberg, circa 1815, a shako of the Louis
Jägers of Württemberg, 1813 (512), an iron Garde du Corps helmet from Württemberg, 1806 (50).
Original description from the catalog.

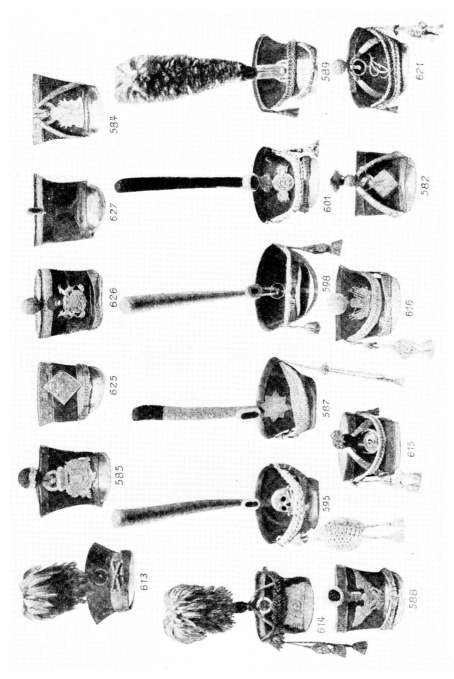

476

476 Reprint from the auction catalog for the Buhrig collection, Leipzig, Hiersemann Co., 1913, showing shakos: Hesse-Darmstadt artillery, circa 1828 (613); Neufchatel Infantry, 1814-48 (585); 2nd Württemberg Cavalry Regiment, 1813 (625); Trumpeter of the 3rd Württemberg Cavalry Regiment, 1815 (626), 1st Württemberg Foot Jäger Battalion, 1806 (627); Infantry of the Canton of Geneva, 1815 (584), Lübeck Home Guard, 1820 (614); 2nd Prussian Hussar Regiment, 1824 (595); 1st Foot Guard Regiment, Prussia, 1815 (587), Prussian Dragoons, 1820 (598), Mounted Artillery, Prussia, 1825 (601); Fusilier officer, Prussia, 1830 (589), Infantry, Prussia, 1815 (588), Infantry, Nassau, 1820 (615); 2nd Nassau Infantry Regiment, 1815 (616); Voltigeur, Canton of Appenzel, 1813 (582); Infantry officer, Saxe-Weimar, 1828 (621). Original descriptions from the catalog.

477

477 Reprint from the catalog of the Centennial Exposition, Breslau 1913 (for the hundredth anniversary of the Battle of Nations at Leipzig): Room 22, with the Carl Hollitzer collection of Vienna. Especially noted in the catalog is the fact that the painter Hollitzer set up his collection in the display himself and did not let anyone handle his collection.

478

480

481

479

Original Photos of the Bonsack Collection, taken circa 1939:

478 Sergeant of the 1st Hussar Life Guard Regiment No. 1 and full dress guard uniform of the Gardes du Corps, both of Prussia.

479 Helmets of the Saxon Gardes du Corps, plus Ducal Saxon crested cavalry helmets.

480 Doublet and bow helmet of a Prussian general with cuirassier's uniform; Ducal Saxon Fusilier shako and doublet; Prussian Hussar and Cuirassier officers' equipment.

481 Another view of the extensive collection, here of various Prussian cavalry uniforms, with a Bavarian M/1879 heavy cavalry helmet rather lost among them.

There are various ways of building up a significant collection of militaria, which naturally depend on the space and finances at one's disposal. In any case, a collection should not be allowed to become a heap of all manner of things, for one soon loses the joy of collecting and the money as well.

The classic military collection is still the collection of helmets. Helmets can be collected independently of uniforms, do not take up as much space, are very decorative and, naturally, also have the highest financial value (this statement must be qualified by stating that the market shows that various individual details of uniforms or equipment may cost considerably more than the helmet that goes with them: One example is an officer's coat with epaulettes from one of the grenadier regiments, with embroidered collar and cuffs, which can easily attain two or three times the price of the appropriate officer's helmet).

Like helmets, effects and equipment can be collected in and of themselves, particularly epaulettes and shoulder pieces with their varying monograms, decorations and colors; likewise cartridge cases, saber sheaths, belts and uniform buttons.

Collections of such individual pieces have their own appeal, just as do the assembling of complete figures, of uniform types, which can be approached from the following angles:

a)Portrayals of the various service arms of the German Army: Infantry, cavalry, artillery, etc., which can also involve chronology.

b)Building up a special collection dealing exclusively with one particular service arm, for example, the Prussian Cuirassiers.

c)An overview of uniform development in a particular army, such as the Royal Bavarian Army, in which one can also concentrate on a particular era.

d)A chronological collection, such as the uniforms of the countries fighting in the Franco-Prussian War or World War I.

e)The preservation of the heritage of a specific person, for example, an officer whose career is known from original documents and whose weapons, uniforms and medals could be assembled, whereby objects that passed out of his hands can be reassembled.

However one builds up a collection, one should not neglect to create the necessary overview through the use of available literature such as lists of rank, regimental histories, books on uniforms, works of military history or original photos.

Visiting various military museums, contact with other collectors, membership in organizations of military hobbyists and research in appropriate government archives are vital to be able to acquire as much data as possible and constantly broaden one's knowledge of the subject. The trade is a definite, important aid in building up a collection; "chance purchases" at flea markets or "one-time opportunities" direct from private parties can be a big help, but one also runs the risk of getting stuck with frauds or rubbish.

Collectors' items will be collected as long as there are buyers for them. The situation is no different with historic weapons, and even among collectors' items such as helmets and uniforms there are falsifications that have attained a high degree of perfection in many areas. Here too, especially as concerns helmets, caution is advised—rare emblems are often copied (in galvanized copper) and attached to original helmets. On the other

482

483

482 Bavaria: Centennial celebration of the Royal Bavarian 1st Heavy Cavalry Regiment "Prince Karl", June 20-22, 1914; Regimental officers in historic Garde du Corps uniforms; 4th from left, Prince Alfons of Bavaria. Original helmets and Pallaches and replicated uniforms were worn.

483 Centennial of the 1st Heavy Cavalry Regiment, Munich. Quadrille of eight ladies and eight officers in uniforms of the 1st Cuirassier Regiment, 1845-1873; at left, Prince Leopold of Bavaria.

hand, entire metal helmets in particular are copied, with all their components such as eagles or lions, chains, cockades and emblems. It is impossible to provide a foolproof method of recognizing such falsifications—only long experience and buying from reputable dealers protects one from losses.

Uniforms themselves, like old textiles in general, cannot be falsified or made anew, since the materials and fabrics used then, such as kersey, twill, duffle, doeskin, eskimo, cashmere, tricot, woolen velvet and silk, in the quality and weave of those days, no longer exist. As a collector, one quickly develops the ability to recognize such old fabrics by feel, look or smell. Yet old originals can be "improved", whether by adding rare epaulettes, shoulder pieces or insignia, changing the buttons or dyeing. Epaulettes with uncommon monograms are often combined nowadays, in which process basic mistakes are often made, especially in combining several monograms, placing the individual insignia or using the wrong size.

Recognizing old additions can be more difficult. At the beginning of the 19th Century, "centenary celebrations" to honor the hundredth birthdays of individuals or anniversaries of regiments or kingdoms, became very frequent. Kaiser Wilhelm II had the "Kassel Fund" established, where numerous complete uniforms from Prussia's glorious past were prepared in order to celebrate the 200th birthday of King Frederick the Great, the 100th anniversary of the Battle of Nations or the 150th anniversary of the Battle of Hohenfriedberg in a worthy way, with parades in historic uniforms. In Saxony, Bavaria and Württemberg too, many "centenary uniforms" were made to celebrate the hundredth anniversaries of the kingdoms.

The quality of these new-made uniforms and helmets was remarkably good, and the work involved was turned over to, among others, the well-known uniform scholar Professor Richard Knötel. It was most important that the new uniforms not only correspond to the originals in appearance, but that the quality of the materials used and the (hand-sewn) seams of the uniforms be appropriate too. It takes a lot of experience to tell these centenary uniforms and helmets from the (naturally very rare) originals of the 18th and early 19th Centuries. Belt buckets and the like, being made of metal, are likewise easy to falsify.

Special emphasis should be placed on a knowledge of the materials. The quality of materials, especially in officers' pieces, can be a big help in recognizing falsifications—the fineness of decorative detail, the workmanship, the gilding or silvering as well as the quality of embroidery or sewing must be examined. The more highly placed the wearer of a uniform, the finer and more elaborate is the quality of workmanship of his clothes. Experience always sharpens the eyes.

The older a helmet of a uniform is, the more clearly signs of wear will show. They can often be made to disappear by cleaning, but one will still be able to recognize that old metal such as brass or silver becomes brittle, almost glassy and breakable. Old metal that has often been polished no longer has sharp edges, the angles are no longer sharp or exact, especially ferrous metals and objects used by enlisted men. Today we have turned farther than ever away from excessive polishing—a normal patina scarcely disturbs the overall appearance of the piece, but often offers the final assurance of originality. Uniforms and equipment made of cloth naturally become more or less dirty or darkened, especially embroidery. An expertly done, protective chemical cleaning (inside a laundry bag) is always the kindest way to handle them—washing with modern detergents or the use of a washing machine is not recommended, since the dyes used in the old days are not colorfast. (Examples of inexpert cleaning are the countless washed-out sergeants' lance banners with their printed emblems all but invisible, or the limp collars of uniforms whose stiff linings have been destroyed by the wrong kind of cleaning.)

Only the layman allows himself to be impressed by a leather helmet that shines everywhere, with all its trim brought to a high polish, scratches and all. The helmet emblems of headgear were matte-gilded or silvered, and only the raised edges were polished; this is how that extraordinary "valuable" effect so admired today came about. When such items are dirtied or darkened, they should be cleaned only with ammonia, lemon juice or coin cleaner, never scrubbed with an automobile chrome polish! Smooth articles such as chains, helmet top plates or frames can be polished protectively, but rather too little than too much. Nowadays headgear is often offered for sale with its metal fittings overly gilded or newly silvered; the term "frosted" says it all, which is to say that a helmet never looked like that before 1918.

The days of the "Old Army" are some seventy years in the past. Scarcely any officers of those days are still alive—even enlisted men who fought in World War I or served in peacetime before 1914 are becoming ever fewer. It is important to preserve the evidence of military history and its prescribed appearance for posterity.

Original cartons and cases for storing helmets and effects, pre-1918.

A List of all Regiments and Independent Battalions in the Old Army

According to the last peacetime status of 1941, including the name of the regiment, the year of establishment, the garrison (I, II, III indicate the first and subsequent battalions, batteries etc.) as well as army corps membership.

For those regiments that were incorporated into the Prussian Army by military accord or annexation, the state origins will be noted with the added names. The way of printing the name, with some terms in parentheses, represents the official way of writing them before 1918.

In the case of line infantry, the army corps membership is indicated by the color of the shoulder pieces as well as the colored pipings around the three outer edges of the sleeve facings.

Army Corps	Shoulder Pieces	Facing Piping
I	white	white
II	white	—
III	red	white
IV	red	—
V	yellow	white
VI	yellow	—
VII	light blue	white
VIII	light blue	—
IX	white	yellow
X	white	light blue
XI	red	yellow
XV	red	light blue
XVI	yellow	yellow
XVII	yellow etc.	light blue
XVIII	light blue	yellow
XX	light blue	light blue
XXI	light green	white

The following army corps were not Prussian and had, in part, special trim and emblems:

XII	Saxony
XIII	Württemberg
XIV	Baden
XIX	Saxony

The order, especially in the Prussian guard corps, does not necessarily correspond to their numerical order, but rather to the order of rank of a regiment as entered in the list of ranks.

Since all the German states except Bavaria were included in the general numbering, this order is retained. The Bavarian army corps and regiments will be listed at the end, according to their own numbering.

Name of Regiment	Founded	Garrison	Corps	
Infantry				
1st Foot Guard Regiment	1688	Potsdam	Guard	
2nd Foot Guard Regiment	1813	Berlin	Guard	
Tsar Alexander Grenadier Guard	1814	Berlin	Guard	Regiment No. 1
Kaiser Franz Grenadier Guard	1814	Berlin	Guard	Regiment No. 2
Fusilier Guard Regiment	1826	Berlin	Guard	
3rd Foot Guard Regiment	1860	Berlin	Guard	
4th Foot Guard Regiment	1860	Berlin	Guard	
Queen Elisabeth Grenadier Guard	1860	Charlottenburg	Guard	Regiment No. 3
Queen Augusta Grenadier Guard	1860	Berlin	Guard	Regiment No. 4
5th Foot Guard Regiment	1897	Spandau	Guard	
Grenadier Guard Regiment No. 5	1897	Spandau	Guard	
Infantry Training Battalion	1819	Potsdam	Guard	
Grenadier Reg. Crown Prince (1st East Prussian) No. 1	1655	Königsberg	1st	
Grenadier Reg. King Friedrich Wilhelm IV (1st Pomeranian) No. 2	1679	Stettin	2nd	
Grenadier Reg. King Friedrich Wilhelm I (2nd E. Prussian) No. 3	1685	Königsberg	1st	
Grenadier Reg. King Friedrich der Grosse (3rd E. Prussian) No. 4	1626	Rastenburg	1st	
Grenadier Reg. King Friedrich I (4th East Prussian) No. 5	1689	Danzig	17th	
Grenadier Reg. Count Kleist von Nollendorf (1st W. Prussian) No. 6	1772	Posen	5th	
Grenadier Reg. King Wilhelm I (2nd West Prussian) No. 7	1797	Liegnitz	5th	
Life Guard Grenadier Reg. King Friedrich Wilhelm III (1st Brandenburg) No. 8	1808	Frankfurt/Oder	3rd	
Colberg Grenadier Reg. Count Gneisenau (2nd Pomeranian) No. 9	1808	Stargard	2nd	
Grenadier Reg. King Friedrich Wilhelm II (1st Silesian) No. 10	1808	Schweidnitz	6th	
Grenadier Reg. King Friedrich III (2nd Silesian) No. 11	1808	Breslau	6th	
Grenadier Reg. Prince Carl of Prussia (2nd Brandenburg) No. 12	1813	Frankfurt/Oder	3rd	
Infantry Reg. Herwarth von Bittenfeld (1st Westphalian) No. 13	1813	Münster	7th	
Inf. Reg. Count Schwerin (3rd Pomeranian) No. 14	1813	Bromberg	2nd	
Inf. Reg. Prince Frederick, of The Netherlands (2nd Westphalian) No. 15	1813	Minden	7th	
Inf. Reg. Baron von Sparr (3rd Westphalian) No. 16	1813	Cologne	7th	
Inf. Reg. Count Barfuss (4th Westphalian) No. 17	1813	Mörchingen	21st	
Inf. Reg. von Grolman (1st Posen) No. 18	1813	Osterode	20th	
Inf. Reg. von Coubière (2nd Posen) No. 19	1813	Görlitz, II Lauban	5th	
Inf. Reg. Count Tauentzien von Wittenberg (3rd Brandenburg) No. 20	1813	Wittenberg	3rd	
Inf. Reg. von Borcke (4th Pomeranian) No. 21	1813	Thorn	17th	
Inf. Reg. Keith (1st Upper Silesian) No. 22	1813	Gleiwitz, III Kattowicz	6th	
Inf. Reg. von Winterfeldt (2nd Upper Silesian) No. 23	1813	Neisse	6th	
Inf. Reg. Grand Duke Friedrich Franz II of Mecklenburg-Schwerin (4th Brandenburg) No. 24	1813	Neu-Ruppin	3rd	
Inf. Reg. von Lützow (1st Rhenish) No. 25	1813	Aachen	8th	
Inf. Reg. Prince Leopold of Anhalt-Dessau (1st Magdeburg) No. 26	1813	Magdeburg	4th	
Inf. Reg. Prince Louis Ferdinand of Prussia (2nd Magdeburg) No. 27	1815	Halberstadt	4th	
Inf. Reg. von Goeben (2nd Rhenish) No. 28 I, II	1813	Ehrenbreitstein Koblenz	8th	
Inf. Reg. von Horn (3rd Rhenish) No. 29	1813	Trier	8th	
Inf. Reg. Count Werder (4th Rhenish) No. 30	1812	Saarlouis	16th	
Inf. Regiment Count Bose (1st Thuringian) No. 31	1812	Altona	9th	
2nd Thuringian Inf. Reg. No. 32	1815	Meiningen	11th	

Name of Regiment	Founded	Garrison	Corps
Fusilier Reg. Count Roon (East Prussian) No. 33	1749	Gumbinnen	1st
Fusilier Reg. Queen Viktoria of Sweden (Pomeranian) No. 34	1720	Stettin, II Swinemünde	2nd
Fusilier Reg. Prince Heinrich of Prussia (Brandenburg) No. 35	1815	Brandenburg	3rd
Fusilier Reg. Field Marshal Count Blumenthal (Magdeburg) No. 36	1815	Halle, II Bernburg	4th
Fusilier Reg. von Steinmetz (West Prussian) No. 37	1818	Lrotoschin	5th
Fusilier Reg. Field Marshal Count Moltke (Silesian) No. 38	1818	Glatz	6th
Lower Rhenish Fusilier Reg. No. 39	1818	Düsseldorf	7th
Fusilier Reg. Prince Karl-Anton of Hohenzollern (Hohenzollern) No. 40	1818	Rastatt	14th
Inf. Reg. von Boyen (5th East Prussian) N0. 41	1860	Tilsit, III Memel	1st
Inf. Reg. Prince Moritz of Anhalt-Anhalt-Dessau (5th Pomeranian) No. 42	1860	Stralsund, III Greifswald	2nd
Inf. Reg. Duke Karl of Mecklenburg-Strelitz (6th East Prussian) No. 43	1860	Königsberg, II Pillau	1st
Inf. Reg. Count Dönhoff (7th East 1st Prussian) No. 44	1860	Goldap	1st
8th East Prussian Inf. Reg. No. 45	1860	Insterburg, I Darkehmen	1st
Inf. Reg. Count Kirchbach (1st Lower Silesian) No. 46	1860	Posen, III Wreschen	5th
Inf. Reg. King Ludwig III of Bavaria (2nd Lower Silesian) No. 47	1860	Posen, II Schrimm	5th
Inf. Reg. von Stülpnagel (5th Brandenburg) No. 48	1860	Cüstrin	3rd
6th Pomeranian Inf. Reg. No. 49	1860	Gnesen	2nd
3rd Lower Silesian Inf. Reg. No. 50	1860	Rawitsch, III Lissa, Breslau	5th
4th Lower Silesian Inf. Reg. No. 51	1860	Breslau	6th
Inf. Reg. von Alvensleven (6th Brandenburg) No. 5	1860	Cottbus, I Crossen	3rd
5th Westphalian Inf. Reg. No. 53	1860	Cologne	7th
Inf. Reg. von der Goltz (7th Pomeranian) No. 54	1860	Kolberg, III Köslin	2nd
Inf. Reg. Count Bülow von Dennewitz (6th Westphalian) No. 55	1860	Detmold, I Höxter, II Bielefeld	7th
Inf. Reg. Vogel von Falckenstein (7th Westphalian) No. 56	1860	Wesel, III Cleve	7th
Inf. Reg. Duke Ferdinand of Braunschweig (8th Westphalian) No. 57	1860	Wesel	7th
3rd Posen Inf. Reg. No. 58	1860	Glogau, III Fraustadt	5th
Inf. Reg. Baron Hiller von Gaertringen (4th Posen) No. 59	1860	Deutsch-Eylau, Soldau	20th
Inf. Reg. Margrave Karl (7th Brandenburg) No. 60	1860	Weissenburg	21st
Inf. Reg. von der Marwitz (8th Pomeranian) No. 61	1860	Thorn	17th
3rd Upper Silesian Inf. Reg. No. 62	1860	Cosel, III Ratibor	6th
4th Upper Silesian Inf. Reg. No. 63	1860	Oppeln, III Lublinitz	6th
Inf. Reg. Field Marshal Prince Friedrich Karl of Prussia (8th Brandenburg) No. 64	1860	Prenzlau, III Angermünde	3rd
5th Rhenish Inf. Reg. No. 65	1860	Cologne	8th
3rd Magdeburg Inf. Reg. No. 66	1860	Megdeburg	4th
4th Magdeburg Inf. Reg. No. 67	1860	Metz	16th
6th Rhenish Inf. Reg. No. 68	1860	Coblenz	8th
7th Rhenish Inf. Reg. No. 69	1860	Trier	8th
8th Rhenish Inf. Reg. No. 70	1860	Saarbrücken	21st
3rd Thuringian Inf. Reg. No. 71	1860	Erfurt, I Sondershausen	11th
4th Thuringian Inf. Reg. No. 72	1860	Torgau, III Eilenburg	4th

Name of Regiment	Founded	Garrison	Corps
Fusilier Reg. Field Marshal Prince Albrecht of Prussia (Hannover) No. 73	1803	Hannover	10th
1st Hannover Inf. Reg. No. 74	1813	Hannover	10th
Bremen Inf. Reg. (1st Hanseatic) No. 75	1866	Bremen, III Stade	9th
Hamburg Inf. Reg. (2nd Hanseatic) No. 76	1866	Hamburg	9th
2nd Hannover Inf. Reg. No. 77	1813	Celle	10th
Inf. Reg. Duke Friedrich Wilhelm of Braunschweig (East Frisian) No. 78	1813	Osnabrück, III Aurich	10th
Inf. Reg. von Voigts-Rhetz (3rd Hannover) No. 79	1838	Hildesheim	10th
Fusilier Reg. von Gerdsdorff (Electoral Hessian) No. 80	1813	Wiesbaden, III Homburg	18th
Inf. Reg. Landgrave Friedrich I of Hesse-Kassel (1st Electoral Hessian) No. 81	1813	Frankfurt am Main	18th
2nd Electoral Hessian Inf. Reg. No. 82	1813	Göttingen	11th
Inf. Reg. von Wittich (3rd Electoral Hessian) No. 83	1813	Kassel, III Arolsen	11th
Inf. Reg. von Manstein (Schleswig) No. 84	1866	Schleswig, II	9th
Inf. Reg. Duke of Holstein (Holstein) No. 85	1866	Rendsburg, III Kiel	9th
Fusilier Reg. Queen (Schleswig-Holstein) No. 86	1966	Flensburg, III Sonderburg	9th
1st Nassau Inf. Reg. No. 87	1809	Mainz	18th
2nd Nassau Inf. Reg. No. 88	1808	Mainz, II Hanau	18th
Grand Ducal Mecklenburg Grenadier Reg. No. 89	1782	Schwerin, II Neustrelitz	9th
Grand Ducal Mecklenburg Fusilier Reg. No. 90 Kaiser Wilhelm	1788	Rostock, II Wismar	9th
Oldenburg Inf. Reg. No. 91	1813	Oldenburg	10th
Anhalt Inf. Reg. No. 93	1807	Dessau, II Zerbst	4th
Inf. Reg. Grand Duke of Saxony (5th Thuringian) No. 94	1762	Weimar, II Eisenach, III. Jena	11th
6th Thuringian Inf. Reg. No. 95	1807	Gotha, II Hildburghausen, III Coburg	11th
7th Thuringian Inf. Reg. No. 96	1702/ I 1897	I & II Gera, III Rudolstadt	11th
1st Upper Rhenish Inf. Reg. No. 97	1881	Saarburg	21st
Metz Inf. Reg. No. 98	1881	Metz	16th
2nd Upper Rhenish Inf. Reg. No. 99	1881	Zabern, III Pfalzburg	15th
Royal Saxon 1st (Life Guard) Grenadier Reg. No. 100	1670	Dresden	12th
Royal Saxon 2nd Grenadier Reg. No. 101 Kaiser Wilhelm, King of Prussia	1670	Dresden	12th
Royal Saxon 3rd Inf. Reg. No. 102 King Ludwig III of Bavaria	1709	Zittau	12th
Royal Saxon Inf. Reg. No. 103	1709	Bautzen	12th
Royal Saxon Inf. Reg. Crown Prince No. 104	1701	Chemnitz	19th
Royal Saxon 6th Inf. Reg. No. 105 King Wilhelm II of Württemberg	1701	Strassburg	19th
Royal Saxon 7th Inf. Reg. King Georg No. 106	1708	Leipzig	19th
Royal Saxon 8th Inf. Reg. Prince Johann Georg No. 107	1708	Leipzig	19th
Royal Saxon Rifle (Fusilier) Reg. Prince Georg No. 108	1809	Dresden	12th
1st Baden Life Guard Grenadier Reg. No. 109	1803	Karlsruhe	14th
2nd Baden Grenadier Reg. Kaiser Wilhelm I No. 110	1852	Mannheim, II Heidelberg	14th
Inf. Reg. Margrave Ludwig Wilhelm (3rd Baden) No. 111	1852	Rastatt	14th
4th Baden Inf. Reg. Prince Wilhelm No. 112	1852	Mülhausen	14th
5th Baden Inf,. Reg. No. 113	1861	Freiburg	14th
6th Baden Inf. Reg. Kaiser Friedrich III No. 114 guard unit at Hohenzollern Castle	1867	Konstanz,	14th
Life Guard Inf. Reg. (1st Grand Ducal Hessian) No. 115	1621	Darmstadt	18th
Inf. Reg. Kaiser Wilhelm (2nd Grand Ducal Hessian) No. 116	1813	Giessen	18th

Name of Regiment	Founded	Garrison	Corps
Inf. Life Guard Reg. Grand Duchess (3rd Grand Ducal Hessian) No. 117	1697	Mainz	18th
Inf. Reg. Prince Carl (4th Grand Ducal Hessian) No. 118	1791	Worms	18th
Grenadier Reg. Queen Olga (1st Württemberg) No. 119	1673	Stuttgart	13th
Inf. Reg. Kaiser Wilhelm, King of Prussia (2nd Württemberg) No. 120	1673	Ulm	13th
Inf. Reg. Old Württemberg (3rd Württemberg) No. 121	1716	Ludwigsburg	13th
Fusilier Reg. Kaiser Franz Joseph of Austria, King of Hungary (4th Württemberg) No. 122	1806	Heilbronn, II Mergentheim	13th
Grenadier Reg. King Karl (5th Württemberg) No. 123	1799	Ulm	13th
Inf. Reg. King Wilhelm I (6th Württemberg) No. 124	1673	Weingarten	13th
Inf. Reg. Kaiser Friedrich. King of Prussia (Württemberg) No. 125	1809	Stuttgart	13th
8th Württemberg Inf. Reg. No. 126 Grand Duke Friedrich of Baden	1716	Strassburg	13th
9th Württemberg Inf. Reg. No. 127	1897	Ulm-Wiblingen	13th
Danzig Inf. Reg. No. 128	1881	Danzig, III Neufahrwasser	17th
3rd West Prussian Inf. Reg. No. 129	1881	Graudenz	17th
1st Lorraine Inf. Reg. No. 130	1881	Metz	16th
2nd Lorraine Inf. Reg. No. 131	1881	Mörchingen	21st
1st Lower Alsatian Inf. Reg. No. 132	1881	Strassburg	15th
Royal Saxon 9th Inf. Reg. No. 133	1881	Zwickau	19th
Royal Saxon 10th Inf. Reg. No. 134	1881	Plauen	19th
3rd Lorraine Inf. Reg. No. 135	1887	Diedenhofen	16th
4th Lorraine Inf. Reg. No. 136	1887	Strassburg	15th
2nd Lower Alsatian Inf. Reg. No. 137	1887	Hagenau	21st
3rd Lower Alsatian Inf. Reg. No. 138	1887	Dieuze	21st
Royal Saxon 11th Inf. Reg. No. 139	1887	Döbeln	19th
4th West Prussian Inf. Reg. No. 140	1890	Hohensalza	2nd
Kulmer Inf. Reg. No. 141	1890	Graudenz, III Strassburg/WP	17th
7th Baden Inf. Reg. No. 142	1890	Mülhausen, II Mühlheim	14th
4th Lower Alsatian Inf. Reg. No. 143	1890	Strassburg, III Mutzig	15th
5th Lorraine Inf. Reg. No. 144	1890	Metz-Diedenhofen	16th
Royal Inf. Reg. (6th Lorraine) No. 145	1890	Metz	16th
1st Masurian Inf. Reg. No. 146	1897	Allenstein	20th
2nd Masurian Inf. Reg. No. 147	1897	Lyck, III Lötzen	20th
5th West Prussian Inf. Reg. No. 148	1897	Elbing-Bromberg, III, Braunsberg	20th
6th West Prussian Inf. Reg. No. 149	1897	Schneidemühl, III Dt. Krone	2nd
1st Ermland Inf. Reg. No. 150	1897	Allenstein	20th
2nd Ermland Inf. Reg. No. 151	1897	Sensburg, II Bischofsburg	20th
German Order Inf. Reg. No. 152	1897	Marienburg, III Stuhm	20th
8th Thuringian Inf. Reg. No, 153	1807	Altenburg, III Merseburg	4th
5th Lower Silesian Inf. Reg. No. 154	1897	Jauer, III Striegau	5th
7th West Prussian Inf. Reg. No. 155	1897	Ostrowo, III Pleschen	5th
3rd Silesian Inf. Reg. No. 156	1897	Beuthen, III Tarnowitz	6th
4th Silesian Inf. Reg. No. 157	1897	Brieg	6th
7th Lorraine Inf. Reg. No. 158	1897	Paderborn, III Senne	7th
8th Lorraine Inf. Reg. No. 159	1897	Mülheim/Ruhr, III Geldern	7th
9th Rhenish Inf. Reg. No. 160	1897	Bonn, I Diez, III Euskirchen	8th
10th Rhenish Inf. Reg. No. 161	1897	Düren, II	8th

Name of Regiment	Founded	Garrison	Corps
		Eschweiler, III, Jülich	
Lübeck Inf, Reg. (3rd Hanseatic)	1897	Lübeck, III Eutin	9th
Schleswig-Holstein Inf. Reg/ No. 163	1897	Neumünster, III Heide	4th
4th Hannover Inf. Reg. No. 164	1813	Hameln, III Holzminden	10th
5th Hannover Inf. Reg. No. 165	1813	Quedlinburg, II Blankenburg	4th
Hesse-Homburg Inf. Reg. No. 166	1897	Bitsch	21st
1st Upper Alsatian Inf. Reg. No, 187	1897	Cassel, III Mühlhausen/Th	11th
5th Grand Ducal Hessian Inf. Reg. No. 168	1897	Offenbach, I Butzbach, III Friedberg/Hesse	18th
8th Baden Inf. Reg. No. 169	1897	Lahr, III Villingen	14th
9th Baden Inf. Reg. No. i70	1897	Offenburg, III Donaueschingen	14th
2nd Upper Alsatian Inf. Reg. No. 171	1897	Colmar	15th
3rd Upper Alsatian Inf. Reg. No. 172	1897	Neubreisach	15th
9th Lorraine Inf. Reg. No. 173	1897	Avold, III Metz	16th
10th Lorraine Inf. Reg. No. 174	1897	Forbach, III Strassburg	21st
8th West Prussian Inf. Reg. No. 175	1897	Graudenz, III Schwetz	17th
9th West Prussian Inf. Reg. No. 176	1897	Kulm, II Thorn	17th
Royal Saxon 12th Inf. Reg. No. 177	1897	Dresden	12th
Royal Saxon 13th Inf. Reg. No. 178	1897	Kamenz	12th
Royal Saxon 14th Inf. Reg. No. 179	1897	Wurzen-Leisnig	19th
10th Württemberg Inf. Reg. No. 180	1897	Tübingen, II Schw. Gmünd	13th
Royal Saxon 15th Inf. Reg. No. 181	1887	Chemnitz, III Glauchau	19th
Royal Saxon 16th Inf. Reg. No. 182	1912	Freiberg	12th

Jäger and Riflemen

Name of Regiment	Founded	Garrison	Corps
Guard Jäger Battalion	1744	Potsdam	Guard
Guard Rifle Battalion	1814	Berlin- Lichterfelde	Guard
Jäger Battalion Count Yorck von Wartenburg (East Prussian) No. 1	1744	Ortelsburg	20th
Jäger Battalion Prince Bismarck (Pomeranian) No. 2	1744	Kulm	17th
Brandenburg Jäger Battalion No. 3	1815	Lübben	3rd
Magdeburg Jäger Battalion No. 4	1815	Naumburg	4th
Jäger Battalion von Neumann (1st Silesian) No. 5	1808	Hirschberg	5th
2nd Silesian Jäger Battalion No. 6	1808	Öls	6th
Westphalian Jäger Battalion No. 7	1815	Bückeburg	7th
Rhenish Jäger Battalion No. 8	1815	Schlettstadt	15th
Lauenburg Jäger Battalion No. 9	1866	Ratzeburg	9th
Hannover Jäger Battalion No. 10	1803	Goslar	10th
Electoral Hessian Jäger Battalion No. 11	1813	Marburg	11th
Royal Saxon 1st Jäger Battalion No. 12	1809	Freiberg	12th
Royal Saxon 2nd Jäger Battalion No. 13	1809	Dresden	12th
Grand Ducal Mecklenburg Jäger Battalion No. 14	1821	Colmar	15th

Machine Gun Units

Name of Regiment	Founded	Garrison	Corps
Guard Machine Gun Unit No. 1	1901	Potsdam	Guard
Guard Machine Gun Unit No. 2	1902	Berlin	Guard
Machine Gun Unit No. 1	1900	Breslau	6th
Machine Gun Unit No. 2	1901	Trier	8th
Machine Gun Unit No. 3	1902	Saarburg	21st
Machine Gun Unit No. 4	1901	Thorn	17th
Machine Gun Unit No. 5	1902	Insterburg	1st
Machine Gun Unit No. 6	1904	Metz	11th
Machine Gun Unit No. 7	1900	Paderborn	7th
Machine Gun Unit No. 8 (Royal Saxon)	1903	Leipzig	19th
Fortress Machine Gun Unit No. 1	1913	Königsberg	1st
Fortress Machine Gun Unit No. 2	1913	Fort Boyen	20th
Fortress Machine Gun Unit No. 3	1913	Graudenz	17th
Fortress Machine Gun Unit No. 4	1913	Graudenz	17th
Fortress Machine Gun Unit No. 5	1913	Thorn	17th

Name of Regiment	Founded	Garrison	Corps	
Fortress Machine Gun Unit No. 6	1913	Posen	5th	
Fortress Machine Gun Unit No. 7	1913	Cologne	8th	
Fortress Machine Gun Unit No. 8	1913	Mainz	18th	
Fortress Machine Gun Unit No. 9	1913	Strassburg	15th	
Fortress Machine Gun Unit No. 10	1913	Mutzig	15th	
Fortress Machine Gun Unit No. 11	1913	Diedenhofen	16th	
Fortress Machine Gun Unit No. 12	1913	Metz	16th	
Fortress Machine Gun Unit No. 13	1913	Metz	16th	
Fortress Machine Gun Unit No. 14	1913	Metz	16th	
Fortress Machine Gun Unit No. 15	1913	Metz	16th	

Cavalry

1. Cuirassiers

Name of Regiment	Founded	Garrison	Corps	
Gardes du Corps Regiment	1740	Potsdam	Guard	
Cuirassier Guard Regiment	1815	Berlin	Guard	
Life Guard Cuirassier Reg. Great Elector (Silesian) No. 1	1674	Breslau	6th	
Cuir. Reg. Queen (Pomeranian) No. 2	1717	Pasewalk	2nd	
Cuir. Reg. Count Wrangel (East Prussian) No. 3	1717	Königsberg	1st	
Cuir. Reg. von Driesen (Westphalian) No. 4	1717	Münster	7th	
Cuir. Reg. Duke Friedrich Eugen of Württemberg (West Prussian) No. 5	1717	Riesenburg, II Rosenberg, III Deutsch-Eylau	20th	
Cuir. Reg. Tsar Nicholas I of Russia (Brandenburg) No. 6	1691	Brandenburg	3rd	
Cuir. Reg. von Seydlitz (Magdeburg) No. 7	1815	I Quedlinburg, II-IV Halberstadt	4th	
Cuir. Reg. Count Gessler (Rhenish) No. 8	1815	Deutz	8th	
Royal Saxon Cavalry Guard Reg. (1st Heavy Reg.)	1680	Dresden	12th	
Royal Saxon Carbine Reg. (2nd Heavy Reg.)	1849	Borna (Leipzig)	19th	

2. Dragoons

Name of Regiment	Founded	Garrison	Corps	Collar and cuff color
1st Dragoon Guard Reg. Queen Victoria of Great Britain & Ireland	1815	Berlin	Guard	red
2nd Dragoon Guard Reg. Empress Alexandra of Russia	1860	Berlin	Guard	red
Dragoon Reg. Prince Albrecht of Prussia (Lithuanian) No. 1	1717	Tilsit	1st	red
1st Brandenburg Dragoon Reg. No. 2	1689	Schwedt/Oder	3rd	black
Mounted Grenadier Reg. Baron von Derfflinger (Neumark) No. 3	1704	Bromberg	2nd	rose
Dragoon Reg. von Bredow (1st Silesian) No. 4	1815	Lüben	5th	yellow
Dragoon Reg. Baron von Manteuffel (Rhenish) No. 5	1860	Hofgeismar	11th	red
Magdeburg Dragoon Reg. No. 6	1860	Mainz	17th	black
Westphalian Dragoon Reg. No. 7	1860	Saarbrücken	21st	rose
Dragoon Reg. King Friedrich III (2nd Silesian) No. 8	1860	Kreuzburg/Bern-stadt/Namslau	6th	yellow
Dragoon Reg. King Carol I of Rumania (1st Hannover) No. 9	1805	Metz	16th	white
Dragoon Reg. King Albert of Saxony (East Prussian) No. 10	1866	Allenstein	20th	white
Dragoon Reg. von Wedel (Pomeranian) No. 11	1866	Lyck	20th	carmine
Dragoon Reg. von Arnim (2nd Brandenburg) No. 12	1866	Gnesen	2nd	carmine
Schleswig-Holstein Dragoon Reg. No. 13	1866	Metz	16th	red
Kurmark Dragoon Reg. No. 14	1866	Colmar	15th	black
3rd Silesian Dargoon Reg. No. 15	1866	Hagenau	15th	rose
2nd Hannover Dragoon Reg. No. 16	1813	Lüneburg	10th	yellow
1st Grand Ducal Mecklenburg Dragoon Reg. No. 17	1819	Ludwigslust	9th	red
2nd Grand Ducal Mecklenburg Dragoon Reg. No. 18	1867	Parchim	9th	black
Oldenburg Dragoon Reg. No, 19	1849	Oldenburg	10th	black
1st Baden Life Guard Dragoon Reg. No. 20	1803	Karlsruhe	14th	red
2nd Baden Dragoon Reg. No. 21	1850	Bruchsal/ Schwetzingen	14th	yellow
3rd Baden Dragoon Reg. Prince Karl No. 22	1850	Mühlhausen	14th	black
Dragoon Guard Reg. (1st Grand Ducal Hessian) No. 23	1790	Darmstadt	18th	red

Name of Regiment	Founded	Garrison	Corps	
Life Guard Dragoon Reg. (2nd Grand Ducal Hessian) No. 24	1859	Darmstadt	18th	white
Dragoon Reg. Queen Olga (1st Württemberg) No. 25	1813	Ludwigsburg	13th	white
Dragoon Reg. King (2nd Württemberg) No. 26 (Cannstadt)	1805	Stuttgart	13th	yellow

3. Hussars

Attila color

Name of Regiment	Founded	Garrison	Corps	
Life Guard Hussar Regiment	1815	Potsdam	Guard	red
1st Life Guard Hussar Reg. No. 1,	1741	Danzig-Langfuhr	17th	black
2nd Life Guard Hussar Reg. Queen Victoria of Prussia No. 2	1741	Danzig-Langfuhr	17th	black
Hussar Reg. von Zieten (Brandenburg) No. 3	1730	Rathenow	3rd	red
Hussar Reg. von Schill (1st Silesian) No. 4	1741	Ohlau	6th	brown
Hussar Reg. Prince Blücher von Wahlstatt (Pomeranian) No. 5	1758	Stolp	17th	red
Hussar Reg. Count Goetzen (2nd Silesian) No. 6	1808	Leobschutz, Ratibor	6th	dark green
Hussar Reg. King Wilhelm I (1st Rhenish) No. 7	1815	Bonn	8th	Russian blue
Hussar Reg. Tsar Nicholas II of Russia (1st Westphalian) No. 8	1815	II & V Paderborn, others Neuhaus	7th	dark blue
2nd Rhenish Hussar Reg. No. 9	1815	Strassburg	15th	blue
Magdeburg Hussar Reg. No. 10	1813	Stendal	4th	dark green
2nd Westphalian Hussar Reg. No. 11,	1813	Krefeld	7th	dark green
Thuringian Hussar Reg. No. 12	1791	Torgau	4th	blue
Hussar Regiment King Umberto of Italy (1st Electoral Hessian) No. 13	1813	Diedenhofen	16th	blue
Hussar Reg. Landgrave Friedrich II of Hesse-Homburg (2nd Electoral Hessian) No. 14	1813	Kassel	11th	dark blue
Hussar Reg. Queen Wilhelmina of The Netherlands (Hannover) No. 15	1803	Wandsbek	9th	blue
Hussar Reg. Kaiser Franz Joseph of Austria, King of Hungary (Schleswig-Holstein) No. 16	1866	Schleswig	9th	dark blue
Braunschweig Hussar Reg. No. 17,	1809	Braunschweig	10th	black
Royal Saxon Hussar Reg. King Albert No. 18	1734	Grossenhain	12th	blue
Royal Saxon 2nd Hussar Reg. No. 19,	1791	Grimma	19th	blue
Royal Saxon 3rd Hussar Reg. No. 20,	1910	Bautzen	12th	field gray

4. Uhlans

Name of Regiment	Founded	Garrison	Corps
1st Uhlan Guard Regiment	1819	Potsdam	Guard
2nd Uhlan Guard Regiment	1819	Berlin	Guard
3rd Uhlan Guard Regiment	1860	Potsdam	Guard
Uhlan Reg. Tsar Alexander III of Russia (West Prussian) No. 1	1745	Militsch-Ostrowo	5th
Uhlan Reg. von Katzler (Silesian) No. 2	1745	Gleiwitz-Pless	6th
Uhlan Reg. Tsar Alexander II of Russia (1st Brandenburg) No. 3	1809	Fürstenwalde	3rd
Uhlan Reg. von Schmidt (1st Pomeranian) No. 4	1815	Thorn	20th
Westphalian Uhlan Reg. No. 5	1815	Düsseldorf	7th
Thuringian Uhlan Reg. No. 6	1813	Hanau	18th
Uhlan Reg. Grand Duke Friedrich of Baden (Rhenish) No. 7	1734	Saarbrücken	21st
Uhlan Reg. Count zu Dohna (East Prussian) No. 8	1812	Gumbinnen-Stallupönen	1st
2nd Pomeranian Uhlan Reg. No. 9	1860	Demmin	2nd
Uhlan Reg. Prince August of Württemberg (Posen) No. 10	1860	Züllichau	5th
Uhlan Reg. Count Haeseler (2nd Brandenburg) No. 11	1860	Saarburg	21st
Lithuanian Uhlan Reg. No. 12	1860	Insterburg	1st
Royal Uhlan Reg. (1st Hannover) No. 13	1803	Hannover	10th
2nd Hannover Uhlan Reg. No. 14	1805	Avold-Mörchingen	16th
Schleswig-Holstein Uhlan Reg. No. 15	1866	Saarburg	21st
Uhlan Reg. Hennigs von Treffenfeld (Altmark) No. 16	1866	Saarburg	21st

Name of Regiment	Founded	Garrison	Corps
Royal Saxon 1st Uhlan Reg. No. 17 Kaiser Franz Joseph of Austria, King of Hungary	1867	Oschatz	12th
Royal Saxon 2nd Uhlan Reg. No. 18	1867	Leipzig	19th
Uhlan Reg. King Karl (1st Württemberg) No. 19	1683	Ulm-Wiblingen	13th
Uhlan Reg. King Wilhelm I (2nd Württemberg) No. 20	1809	Ludwigsburg	13th
Royal Saxon 3rd Uhlan Reg. No. 21 Kaiser Wilhelm II, King of Prussia	1905	Chemnitz	19th

5. Mounted Jäger

Name of Regiment	Founded	Garrison	Corps
Royal Mounted Jäger Reg. No. 1	1905	Posen	5th
Mounted Jäger Reg. No. 2	1905	Langensalza	11th
Mounted Jäger Reg. No. 3	1905	Colmar	15th
Mounted Jäger Reg. No. 4	1906	Graudenz	17th
Mounted Jäger Reg. No. 5	1908	Mülhausen	14th
Mounted Jäger Reg. No. 6	1910	Erfurt	11th
Mounted Jäger Reg. No. 7	1913	Trier	8th
Mounted Jäger Reg. No. 8	1913	Trier	8th
Mounted Jäger Reg. No. 9	1913	Insterburg	1st
Mounted Jäger Reg. No. 10	1913	Angerburg-Goldap	1st
Mounted Jäger Reg. No. 11	1913	Tarnowitz-Lublinitz	6th
Mounted Jäger Reg. No. 12	1913	Avold	16th
Mounted Jäger Reg. No. 13	1913	Saarlouis	16th

Field Artillery

Name of Regiment	Founded	Garrison	Corps
1st Field Artillery Guard Regiment	1816	Berlin	Guard
2nd Field Artillery Guard Regiment	1872	Potsdam	Guard
3rd Field Artillery Guard Regiment	1899	Berlin-Beeskow	Guard
4th Field Artillery Guard Regiment	1899	Potsdam	Guard
F. A. Reg. Prince August of Prussia (1st Lithuanian) No. 1	1772	Gumbinnen-Insterburg	1st
1st Pomeranian F. A. Reg. No. 2	1808	Kolberg-Belgard	2nd
F. A. Reg. Ordnance General (1st Brandenburg) No. 3	1816	Brandenburg	3rd
F. A. Reg. Prince Regent Luitpold of Bavaria (Magdeburg) No. 4	1816	Magdeburg	4th
F. A. Reg. von Podbielski (1st Lower Silesian) No. 5	1816	Sprottau-Sagan	5th
F. A. Reg. von Peucker (1st Silesian) No. 6	1808	Breslau	6th
1st Westphalian F. A. Reg. No. 7	1816	Wesel-Düsseldorf	7th
F. A. Reg. von Holtzendorff (1st Rhenish) No. 8	1816	Saarbruucken	21st
F. A. Reg. Field Marshal Count Waldersee (Schleswig) No. 9	1866	Itzehoe	9th
	1866	Itzehoe	19th
F. A. Reg. von Scharnhorst (1st Hannover) No. 10	1803	Hannover	10th
1st Electoral Hessian F. A. Reg.	1813	Cassel-Fritzlar	11th
Royal Saxon 1st F. A. Reg. No. 12	1620	Dresden-Königsbrück	12th
F. A. Reg. King Karl (1st Württemberg) No. 13	1736	Ulm-Stuttgart	13th
F. A. Reg. Grand Duke (1st Baden) No. 14	1850	Karlsruhe	14th
1st Upper Alsatian F. A. Reg. No. 15	1871	Saarburg-Mörchingen	21st
1st East Prussian F. A. Reg. No. 16	1872	Königsberg	1st
2nd Pomeranian F. A. Reg. No. 17	1872	Bromberg	2nd
F. A. Reg. Ordnance General (2nd Brandenburg) No. 18	1872	Frankfurt/Oder	11th
1st Thuringian F. A. Reg. No. 19	1872	Erfurt	11th
1st Posen F. A. Reg. No. 20	1872	Posen	5th
F. A. Reg. von Clausewitz (1st Upper Silesian) No. 21	1872	Neisse-Grottkau	6th
2nd Westphalian F. A. Reg. No. 22	1872	Münster	7th
2nd Rhenish F. A. Reg. No. 23	1872	Koblenz	8th
Holstein F. A. Reg. No. 24	1872	Güstrow-Neustrelitz	9th
Grand Ducal Art. Corps, 1st Grand Ducal Hessian F. A. Reg. No. 25	1790	Darmstadt	18th

Name of Regiment	Founded	Garrison	Corps
2nd Hannover F. A. Reg. No. 26	1872	Verden	10th
1st Nassau F. A. Reg. No. 27	1833	Mainz-Wiesbaden	18th
Royal Saxon 2nd F. A. Reg. No. 28	1872	Bautzen	12th
2nd Württemberg F. A. Reg. No. 29 Prince Regent Luitpold of Bavaria	1736	Ludwigsburg	13th
2nd Baden F. A. Reg. No. 30	1872	Rastatt	14th
1st Lower Alsatian F. A. Reg. No. 31	1881	Hagenau	21st
Royal Saxon 3rd F. A. Reg. No. 32	1889	Riesa	19th
1st Lorraine F. A. Reg. No. 33	1890	Metz	16th
2nd Lorraine F. A. Reg. No. 24	1890	Metz	16th
1st West Prussian F. A. Reg. No. 35	1890	Deutsch-Eylau	20th
2nd West Prussian F. A. Reg. No. 36	1890	Danzig	17th
2nd Lithuanian F. A. Reg. No. 37	1899	Insterburg	1st
Near Pomeranian F. A. Reg. No. 38	1899	Stettin	2nd
Kurmark F. A. Reg. No. 39	1899	Perleberg	3rd
Altmark F. A. Reg. No. 40	1899	Burg	4th
2nd Lower Silesian F. A. Reg. No. 41	1899	Glogau	5th
2nd Silesian F. A. Reg. No. 42	1899	Schweidnitz	6th
Cleves F. A. Reg. No. 43	1899	Wesel	7th
Trier F. A. Reg. No. 44	1899	Trier	8th
Lauenburg F. A. Reg. No. 45	1899	Altona-Rendsburg	9th
Lower Saxon F. A. Reg. No. 46	1899	Wolfenbüttel-Celle	10th
2nd Electoral Hessian F. A. Reg. No. 47	1899	Fulda	11th
Royal Saxon 4th F. A. Reg. No. 48	1899	Dresden	12th
3rd Württemberg F. A. Reg. No. 49	1899	Ulm	13th
3rd Baden F. A. Reg. No. 50	1899	Karlsruhe	14th
2nd Upper Alsatian F. A. Reg. No. 51	1899	Strassburg	15th
2nd East Prussian F. A. Reg. No. 52	1899	Königsberg	1st
Far Pomeranian F. A. Reg. No. 53	1899	Bromberg-Hohensalza	2nd
Neumark F. A. Reg. No. 54	1899	Cüstrin	3rd
2nd Thuringian F. A. Reg. No. 55	1899	Naumburg	11th
2nd Posen F. A. Reg. No. 56	1899	Lissa	5th
2nd Upper Silesian F. A. Reg. No. 57	1899	Neustadt/Oberschl.	6th
Minden F. A. Reg. No. 58	1899	Minden	7th
Berg F. A. Reg. No. 59	1899	Cologne	8th
Grand Ducal Mecklenburg F. A. Reg. No. 60	1899	Schwerin	9th
2nd Grand Ducal Hessian F. A. Reg. No. 61	1899	Darmstadt-Babenhausen	18th
East Frisian F. A. Reg. No. 62	1899	Oldenburg-Osnabrück	10th
2nd Nassau F. A. Reg. No. 63	1899	Frankfurt	18th
Royal Saxon 5th F. A. Reg. No. 64	1901	Pirna	12th
4th Württemberg F. A. Reg. No. 65	1899	Ludwigsburg	13th
4th Baden F. A. Reg. No. 66	1899	Lahr	15th
2nd Lower Alsatian F. A. Reg. No. 67	1899	Hagenau-Bischweiler	21st
Royal Saxon 6th F. A. Reg. No. 68	1899	Riesa	19th
3rd Lorraine F. A. Reg. No. 69	1899	St. Avold	16th
4th Lorraine F. A. Reg. No. 70	1899	Metz-Saarlouis	16th
F. A. Reg. No. 71 Gross-Komtur	1899	Graudenz	17th
F. A. Reg. No. 72 Hochmeister	1899	Marienwerder-Stargard	17th
1st Masurian F. A. Reg. No. 73	1899	Allenstein	20th
Torgau F. A. Reg. No. 74	1899	Torgau-Wittenberg	4th
Mansfeld F. A. Reg. No. 75	1899	Halle	4th
5th Baden F. A. Reg. No. 76	1899	Freiburg	14th
Royal Saxon 7th F. A. Reg. No. 77	1899	Leipzig	19th
Royal Saxon 8th F. A. Reg. No. 78	1901	Wurzen	19th
3rd East Prussian F. A. Reg. No. 79	1912	Osterode	20th
3rd Upper Alsatian F. A. Reg. No. 80	1912	Colmar-Neubreisach	15th
Thorn F. A. Reg. No. 81	1912	Thorn	17th
1nd Masurian F. A. Reg. No. 82	1912	Rastenburg-Lötzen	20th
3rd Rhenish F. A. Reg. No. 83	1912	Bonn-Düren	8th
Strassburg F. A. Reg. No. 84	1912	Strassburg	15th
Field Artillery Gunnery School	1867	Jüterbog	Guard

Foot Artillery

Ft. Artillery Guard Regiment	1865	Spandau	Guard
Ft. A. Reg. von Linger (East Prussian) No. 1	1864	Königsberg	1st
Ft. A. Reg. von Hindersin (1st Pomeranian) No. 2	1865	Swinemünde-Emden	2nd
Ft. A. Reg. Ordnance General (Brandenburg) No. 3	1864	Mainz	18th

Name of Regiment	Founded	Garrison	Corps
Ft. A. Reg. Encke (Magdeburg) No. 4	1864	Magdeburg	4th
Lower Silesian Ft. A. Reg. No. 5	1865	Posen	5th
Ft. A. Reg. von Dieskau (Silesian) No. 6	1865	Neisse-Glogau	6th
Westphalian Ft. A. Reg. No. 7	1864	Cologne	7th
Rhenish Ft. A. Reg. No. 8	1864	Metz	16th
Schleswig-Holstein Ft. A. Reg. No. 9	1893	Ehrenbreitstein	8th
Lower Saxon Ft. A. Reg. No. 10	1871	Strassburg	15th
1st West Prussian Ft. A. Reg. No. 11	1881	Thorn	17th
1st Royal Saxon Ft. A. Reg. No. 12	1873	Metz	19th
Hohenzollern Ft. A. Reg. No. 13	1805	Ulm-Breisach	15th
Baden Ft. A. Reg. No. 14	1893	Strassburg	14th
2nd Pomeranian Ft. A. Reg. No. 15	1893	Bromberg-Graudenz	2nd
Lorraine Ft. A. Reg. No. 16	1912	Metz-Diedenhofen	16th
2nd West Prussian Ft. A. Reg. No. 17	1911	Danzig-Pillau	17th
Thuringian Ft. A. Reg. No. 18	1912	Niederzwehren (Kassel)	11th
2nd Royal Saxon Ft. A. Reg. No. 19	1912	Dresden-Riesa	12th
Lauenburg Ft. A. Reg. No. 20	1912	Altona	9th
Foot Artillery Gunnery School	1867	Jüterbog	Guard
Senior Ordnance Sergeants' School	1840	Berlin	—
Artillery Testing Commission	1809	Berlin	War Ministry

Engineers

Name of Regiment	Founded	Garrison	Corps
Engineer Guard Battalion	1810	Berlin	Guard
Eng. Batt. Prince Radziwill (East Prussian) No. 1	1780	Königsberg	1st
Pomeranian Eng. Batt. No. 2	1816	Stettin	2nd
Eng. Batt. von Rauch (1st Brandenburg) No. 3	1741	Spandau	3rd
Magdeburg Eng. Batt. No. 4	1816	Magdeburg	4th
Lower Silesian Eng. Batt. No. 5	1816	Glogau	5th
Silesian Eng. Batt. No. 6	1816	Neisse	6th
1st Westphalian Eng. Batt. No. 7	1816	Cologne	7th
1st Rhenish Eng. Batt. No. 8	1816	Koblenz	8th
Schleswig-Holstein Eng. Batt. No. 9	1866	Harburg	9th
Hannover Eng. Batt. No. 10	1804	Minden	10th
Electoral Hessian Eng. Batt. No. 11	1842	Hann.-Münden	11th
Royal Saxon 1st Eng. Batt. No. 12	1698	Pirna	12th
Württemberg Eng. Batt. No. 13	1814	Ulm	13th
Baden Eng. Batt. No. 14	1850	Kehl	14th
1st Alsatian Eng. Batt. No. 15	1871	Strassburg	15th
1st Lorraine Eng. Batt. No. 16	1881	Metz	16th
1st West Prussian Eng. Batt. No. 17	1890	Thorn	17th
Samland Eng. Batt. No. 18	1893	Königsberg	1st
2nd Alsatian Eng. Batt. No. 19	1893	Strassburg	15th
2nd Lorraine Eng. Batt. No. 20	1893	Metz	16th
1st Nassau Eng. Batt. No. 21	1901	Mainz	18th
Royal Saxon 2nd Eng. Batt. No. 22	1899	Riesa	19th
2nd West Prussian Eng. Batt. No. 23	1907	Graudenz	20th
2nd Westphalian Eng. Batt. No. 24	1908	Cologne	7th
2nd Nassau Eng. Batt. No. 25	1909	Mainz	18th
Masurian Eng. Batt. No. 26	1912	Graudenz	20th
2nd Rhenish Eng. Batt. No. 27	1912	Trier	21st
2nd Brandenburg Eng. Batt. No. 28	1913	Cüstrin	3rd
Posen Eng. Batt. No. 29	1913	Posen	5th
3rd Rhenish Eng. Batt. No. 30	1913	Ehrenbreitstein	8th

Transportation & Communication Troops

Name of Regiment	Founded	Garrison	Corps
Railway Regiment No. 1	1875	Berlin	Guard
Railway Regiment No. 2	1890	Hanau	18th
Railway Regiment No. 3	1893	Hanau	18th
Railway Regiment No. 4	1913	Berlin	Guard
Telegraph Battalion No. 1	1899	Berlin	Guard
Telegraph Battalion No. 2	1899	Frankfurt/Oder-Cottbus	3rd
Telegraph Battalion No. 3	1899	Koblenz-Darmstadt	8th
Telegraph Battalion No. 4	1907	Karlsruhe-Freiburg	14th
Telegraph Battalion No. 5	1912	Danzig	17th
Telegraph Battalion No. 6	1913	Hannover	10th
Royal Saxon Telegraph Batt. No. 7	1913	Dresden	12th
War Telegraph School	1913	Spandau	Guard
Airship Battalion No. 1	1884	Berlin	Guard

Name of Regiment	Founded	Garrison	Corps
Airship Battalion No. 2	1911	Berlin-Dresden	Guard
Airship Battalion No. 3	1911	Cologne-Düsseldorf	8th
Airship Battalion No. 4	1913	Mannheim-Metz	14th
Airship Battalion No. 5	1913	Graudenz	1st

Aircraft Battalions No. 1 to 4 existed very briefly, being established in June-July 1913 and disbanded on October 1, 1913.

Motor Vehicle Battalion	1911	Berlin	Guard
Test Unit of Military Transportation	1890	Berlin	Guard

Supply Trains

Name of Regiment	Founded	Garrison	Corps
Guard Train Battalion	1853	Berlin	Guard
East Prussian Train Battalion No. 1	1856	Königsberg	1st
Pomeranian Train Batt. No. 2	1853	Alt-Damm	2nd
Brandenburg Train Battalion No. 3	1853	Spandau	3rd
Maghdeburg Train Battalion No. 4	1853	Magdeburg	4th
Lower Silesian Train Battalion No. 5	1853	Posen	5th
Silesian Train Battalion No. 6	1853	Breslau	6th
Westphalian Train Battalion No. 7	1853	Münster	7th
1st Rhenish Train Battalion No. 8	1853	Koblenz	8th
Schleswig-Holstein Train Batt. No. 9	1866	Rendsburg	9th
Hannover Train Battalion No. 10	1866	Hannover	10th
Electoral Hessian Train Batt. No. 11	1854	Kassel	11th
Royal Saxon 1st Train Batt. No. 12	1849	Dresden-Bischofswerda	12th
Württemberg Train Battalion No. 13	1871	Ludwigsburg	13th
Baden Train Battalion No. 14	1864	Durlach	14th
Alsatian Train Battalion No. 15	1871	Strassburg	15th
Lorraine Train Battalion No. 16	1890	Saarlouis	16th
West Prussian Train Batt. No. 17	1890	Danzig-Langfuhr	17th
Grand Ducal Hessian Train Battalion No. 18	1890	Darmstadt	18th
Royal Saxon Train Battalion No. 19	1899	Leipzig	19th
Masurian Train Battalion No. 20	1912	Marienburg	20th
2nd Rhenish Train Battalion No. 21	1912	Forbach	21st

Royal Bavarian Army
Commander-in-Chief: His Majesty King Ludwig III

Infantry

The shoulder flaps of the infantry regiments in all three army corps were red, the sleeve panel edgings: 1st Corps: white, 2nd Corps: none, 3rd Corps: yellow. Corps listed below are Bavarian.

Name of Regiment	Founded	Garrison	Corps
Infantry Life Guard Regiment	1814	Munich	1st
1st Infantry Regiment King	1778	Munich	1st
2nd Infantry Regiment Crown Prince	1682	Munich	1st
3rd Inf. Reg. Prince Karl of Bavaria	1698	Augsburg	1st
4th Inf. Reg. King Wilhelm of Württemberg	1706	Metz	2nd
5th Inf. Reg. Grand Duke Ernst Ludwig of Hesse	1722	Bamberg	2nd
6th Inf. Reg. Kaiser Wilhelm, King of Prussia	1725	Amberg	3rd
7th Inf. Reg. Prince Leopold	1732	Bayreuth	3rd
8th Inf. Reg. Grand Duke Friedrich II	1753	Metz	2nd
9th Infantry Regiment Wrede	1803	Würzburg	2nd
10th Inf. Reg. King (until 1913 Prince Ludwig)	1682	Ingolstadt	3rd
11th Inf. Reg. von der Tann	1805	Regensburg	3rd
12th Inf. Reg. Prince Arnulf	1814	Neu-Ulm	1st
13th Inf. Reg. Franz Joseph I, Kaiser of Austria, King of Hungary	1806	Ingolstadt, III Eichstätt	3rd
14th Inf. Reg. Hartmann	1814	Nürnberg	3rd
15th Inf. Reg. King August of Saxony	1722	Neuburg/Donau	1st
16th Inf. Reg. Grand Duke Ferdinand of Tuscany	1878	Passau, I Landshut	1st
17th Inf. Reg. Orff	1878	Germersheim	1st
18th Inf. Reg. Prince Ludwig Ferdinand	1881	Landau	2nd
19th Inf. Reg. King Victor Emanuel III of Italy	1890	Erlangen	3rd
20th Inf. Reg. Prince Franz	1897	Lindau, II Kempten	1st
21st Inf. Reg. Grand Duke Friedrich Franz IV of Mecklenburg-Schwerin	1897	Fürth, II Sulzbach	3rd

Name of Regiment	Founded	Garrison	Corps
22nd Infantry Regiment	1897	Zweibrücken	2nd
23rd Infantry Regiment	1897	Landau, II Saargemünd, III Lechfeld Camp	2nd

Jäger

1st Jäger Battalion King	1815	Freising	1st
2nd Jäger Battalion	1753	Aschaffenburg	2nd

Machine Gun Unit

1st Machine Gun Unit (assigned to the 18th Infantry Regiment)	1913	Landau	2nd

Cavalry

1st Heavy Cav. Reg. Prince Karl of Bavaria	1814	Munich	1st
2nd Heavy Cav. Reg. Archduke Franz Ferdinand of Austria-Este	1815	Landshut	1st
1st Uhlan Reg. Kaiser Wilhelm II, King of Prussia	1863	Bamberg	2nd
2nd Uhlan Regiment King	1863	Ansbach	2nd
1st Light Cav. Reg. Tsar Nicholas of Russia	1682	Nürnberg	3rd
2nd Light Cavalry Reg. Taxis	1682	Regensburg	3rd
3rd Light Cav. Reg. Duke Karl Theodor	1724	Dieuze	2nd
4th Light Cav. Reg. King	1744	Augsburg	1st
5th Light Cav. Reg. Archduke Friedrich of Austria	1776	Saargemünd	2nd
6th Light Cav. Reg. Prince Albrecht of Prussia	1803	Bayreuth	3rd
7th Light Cav. Reg. Prince Alfons	1905	Straubing	3rd
8th Light Cavalry Regiment	1909	Dillingen	1st

Field Artillery

1st F. A. Reg. Prince Regent Luitpold	1824	Munich	1st
2nd F. A. Reg. Horn	1824	Würzburg	2nd
3rd F. A. Reg. Prince Leopold	1848	Grafenwöhr	3rd
4th F. A. Reg. King	1859	Augsburg	1st
5th F. A. Reg. King Alfonso XIII of Spain	1890	Landau	2nd
6th F. A. Reg. Prince Ferdinand of Bourbon, Duke of Calabria	1900	Fürth	3rd
7th F. A. Reg. Prince Regent Luitpold	1900	Munich	1st
8th F. A. Reg. Prince Heinrich of Prussia	1900	Nürnberg	3rd
9th Field Artillery Regiment	1901	Landsberg	1st
10th Field Artillery Regiment	1901	Erlangen	3rd
11th Field Artillery Regiment	1901	Würzburg	2nd
12th Field Artillery Regiment	1901	Landau/Pfalz	2nd

Foot Artillery

1st Foot Artillery Reg. (vacant)	1873	Munich, I Neu-Ulm	1st
2nd Foot Artillery Regiment	1873	Metz	2nd
3rd Foot Artillery Regiment	1912	Ingolstadt	3rd

Engineers

1st Engineer Battalion	1900	Munich	1st
2nd Engineer Battalion	1872	Speyer	2nd
3rd Engineer Battalion	1872	Ingolstadt	2nd
4th Engineer Battalion	1912	Ingolstadt	3rd

Transportation and Communication Troops

Railway Battalion	1873	Munich	1st
1st Telegraph Battalion	1901	Munich	1st
2nd Telegraph Battalion	1912	Munich	1st
Aircraft & Motor Vehicle Battalion	1911	Munich	1st
Aircraft Battalion	1911	Ober-Schleissheim	1st

Name of Regiment	Founded	Garrison	Corps
Supply Train			
1st Train Battalion	1872	Munich	1st
2nd Train Battalion	1872	Würzburg, III	2nd
		Germersheim	
3rd Train Battalion	1900	Fürth, I	3rd
		Ingolstadt	

The Federal States of the German Empire as of 1871

4 Kingdoms
6 Grand Duchies
5 Duchies
7 Principalities
3 Free Cities
(with names of rulers or mayors in office before the outbreak of World War I.)

German Emperor: Wilhelm II, King of Prussia (since 1888)

Kingdoms
Prussia (Wilhelm II, since 1888)
Bavaria (Ludwig III, regent, then king, since 1913)
Saxony (Friedrich August III, since 1904)
Württemberg (Wilhelm II, since 1891)

Grand Duchies
Baden (Friedrich II, since 1907)
Hesse-Darmstadt (Ernst Ludwig, since 1892)
Mecklenburg-Schwerin (Friedrich Franz IV, since 1897)
Mecklenburg-Strelitz (Adolf Friedrich VI, since 1914)
Saxe-Weimar (Wilhelm Ernst, since 1901)
Oldenburg (Friedrich August, since 1900)

Duchies
Anhalt (Friedrich II, since 1904)
Braunschweig (Regent Johann Albrecht, since 1907; Ernst August 1913)
Saxe-Altenburg (Ernst II, since 1908)
Saxe-Coburg and Gotha (Karl Eduard, since 1900)
Saxe-Meiningen (Georg, since 1866, to 6/25/1914, succeeded by Bernhard III)

Principalities
Lippe-Detmold (Leopold IV, since 1905)
Reuss elder line (Heinrich XXIV, since 1902)
Reuss younger line (Heinrich XXVII, since 1902)
Schaumburg-Lippe (Adolf, since 1911)
Schwarzburg-Rudolstadt (Günther, since 1890)
Schwarzburg-Sondershausen (Karl Günther to 1909, then Günther, as above, in personal union)
Waldeck-Pyrmont (Friedrich, since 1893)

Free Cities
Bremen (Dr. Barkhausen, Senate President)
Hamburg (Dr. C. A. Schröder, First Mayor)
Lübeck (J. H. Eschenburg, Presiding Mayor)

The Most Important Military Museums in Europe

The collector should avail himself of the opportunity of getting acquainted with the objects in the military museums. This is the best and simplest method of sharpening one's eyes through regular comparison and observation and learning to separate the wheat from the chaff. Here is a list of the most important military museums in Germany and Europe:

Austria
Heergeschlchtliches Museum Wien, Arsenal Objekt 18, Vienna III
Waffensammlung des Kunsthistorischen Museums, Neue Burg, Vienna Landeszeughaus Graz, Steiermark

Belgium
Musée Royal l'Armée et d'Histoire Militaire, Palais du Cinquantenair, Brussels

Bulgaria
Centralnogo Museja Narodnoi Armii, Skobelev, Boulevard 23, Sofia

Czechoslovakia
Vojenské Muzeum, U. Památniku 2, Prag 3

Denmark
Tojhusmuseet, Frederiksholms Kanal 29, Copenhagen

Finland
Militäremuseum, Maurinhatu 3, 00170 Helsinki 17

France
Musée de l'Armée, Hôtel National des Invalides, Paris 7e
Musée de la Marine, Palais de Chaillot, Place du Trocadero, Paris
Musée International des Hussards, Jardin Massey, 65 Tarbes (Hautes-Pyrénées)
Musée Historique de la Ville de Strasbourg, 2 Place du Château, Strasbourg

Germany (West)
Wehrgeschichtliches Museum, Schloss, 7550 Rastatt, Baden
Bayerisches Armeemuseum, Neues Schloss, 8070 Ingolstadt
Festungsund Waffengeschichtliches Museum, 7522 Philippsburg I
Kavallerie-Museum Vornholz, Schloss, 4743 Ostenfelde in Westfalen
Militär-Museum Schloss Bartenstein, 7181 Bartenstein, Württemberg
Luftwaffen-Museum Uetersen, 2082 Uetersen

Germany (East)
Museum für deutsche Geschichte (former Zeughaus of Berlin), X-108 Berlin

Great Britain
National Army Museum, Royal Hospital Road, London SW3 4HT
Imperial War Museum, Lambeth Road, London SE1
Royal Air Force Museum, London
Royal Marines Museum, 22351 Portsmouth

Hungary
Hadtörténelmi Muzeum, I. Tóth Arpád sétány (Promenade) No. 40, Budapest

Italy
Museo Nazionale della Montagna "Duca degli Abruzzi", Via E. Giordano No. 37, 10131 Torino
Museo Nazionale Storico d'Artiglieria, Corso Galileo Ferraris, Torino
Museo Storico dei Bersaglieri, Piazza Porta Pia, Rome
Museo Nazionale di Castel Sant' Angelo, Lungotevere Castello, Rome
Museo Storico dell' Arma dei Carabinieri, Piazza del Risorgimento No. 46, Rome

The Netherlands
Königlich Niederländisches Armeemuseum, Korte Geer 1, Delft
Maritim-Museum, Amsterdam
Luftfahrt-Museum, Soesterberg

Norway
Haermuseet, Akershus, Oslo 1

Poland
Muzeum Wojska Polskiego, Al. Jerozolimskie 3, Warsaw

Rumania
Muzeul Militar Central, Izvor Street 137, Bucharest

Sweden
Kungl. Armémuseum, Riddargatan 13, Stockholm

Soviet Union
Voenno-Istoritjeskij Musej Artillerij, Insjenernich Woisk i Woisk Swjasi, Lenin's Park 7, Leningrad
Centralnij Musej Vooruzhennijch Sil SSSR, Municipal Square 2, Moscow

Spain
Museo Militar del Castillo de Montjuich, Barcelona 4

Switzerland
Musée Historique, Château de Colombier, CH-2013 Colombier
Historisches Museum, Rathaus am Kornmarkt, CH-6000 Luzern
Musée Militaire, Château, CH-1110 Morges
Altes Zeughaus Solothurn, Zeughausplatz 1, CH-4500 Solothurn
Waffen- und Trophäensammlung des Unteroffiziervereins, Hauptgasse 68, CH-4500 Solothurn
Schweizerisches Landesmuseum, Museumstrasse 2, CH-8000 Zürich

Yugoslavia
Vojni Muzej, Kalemagdan, Belgrade

von Alt, *Geschichte der Königlichen Preussischen Kürassiere und Dragoner seit 1619 resp. 1631-1870*, Berlin 1870.

Asbrand, gen. von Porbeck, Viktor, *Geschichte des Königlichen Preussischen Garde-Fuss-Artillerie-Regiments, seiner Stammtruppenteile und Stämme*, Berlin 1885.

Baer, Ludwig, *Die Geschichte des deutschen Stahlhelms von 1915 bis 1945*, Eschborn 1977.

(Bayern): *Bekleidungsvorschrift für die Offiziere, Sanitätsoffiziere und Beamten des Königlichen Bayerischen Heeres*, Munich 1904.

—*Die Feldgraue Friedensund Kriegsbekleidung der Königlichen Bayerischen Armee*, Munich 1916.

—*Bekleidungsordnung*, Munich, 1904.

—*Militär-Handbuch des Königreiches Bayern*, Munich, various editions.

Behringer, Ludwig, *Die Bayerische Armee, König Maximilian II*, Munich 1854, with lithographs by L. Behringer.

von Blankenhorn, Erich, *Führer durch das Historische Museum, Schloss Rastatt, 3 Vol.*, 1960-1962.

Bleckwenn, Dr. Hans, *Die Friderizianischen Uniformen 1753-1786, 4 Vol.*, Osnabrück 1984.

—*Das Altpreussische Heer, Erscheinungsbild und Wesen 1713-1807, 8 Vol.*, Osnabrück 1971.

—*Unter dem Preussen-Adler, Das Brandenburgisch-Preussische Heer 1640-1807*, Munich 1978.

Bluth, Oskar, *Uniform und Tradition*, Berlin 1956.

von Boeheim, W., *Handbuch der Waffenkunde*, Leipzig 1890.

von Brand, Eckert H., *Freiherr, Kadetten, Aus 300 Jahren deutscher Kadettenkorps, Vol. I*, Munich 1981.

Brauer, Hans M. & Knötel, H., *Uniformbogen und Fahnentafeln, Fortlaufende Beiträge zur Uniformkunde, Taktik und Kriegsgeschichte*, Berlin 1926-1932.

Braun, Louis & Müller, Karl, *Die Organisation, Bewaffnung und Ausrüstung der Königlichen Bayerischen Armee von 1806 bis 1906*, Text and Tables, Munich, n.d.

Bredow-Wedel, *Historische Rangund Stammliste des deutschen Heeres*, Berlin 1905; Reprint Verlag Olmes, Krefeld 1974.

(Breslau) *Historische Ausstellung Breslau*, Katalog, Breslau 1913.

(Coburg) *Kunstsammlungen der Veste Coburg*, selected works, Coburg 1969ff.

Damerau, H. & G., *Deutsches Soldatenjahrbuch*, Munich 1954ff.

Deiss, F. W., *Das Deutsche Soldatenbuch*, Berlin 1928.

Der Bunte Rock 1800-1863, Zigarettenbilderalbum, eine Sammlung deutscher Uniformen des 19. Jahrhunderts, Verlag Haus Neuerburg, Cologne, n.d.

(Deutsche Reich) *Deutsche Heeres-Uniformen auf der Weltausstellung in Paris 1900*, Catalog.

Dienstvorschrift für die Königliche Leibgarde der Hartschiere, Munich 1915.

Dresden Historisches Museum (Ed.), *Führer durch des Königliche Historische Museum*, Dresden 1899.

Eckert, F. & Monten, D., *Das Deutsche Bundesheer*, Frankfurt 1845, Reprint Osnabrück 1981.

Eisenhart-Rothe, Ernst & Schauwecker, Franz, *So war die alte Armee*, Berlin 1935.

Farmbacher, Hans, *Führer durch das Königliche Bayerische Armeemuseum*, Munich 1909, with tables, Verlag Wacker, 1912.

Feichtner, Carl, *Bayerische Bürgermilitär und Gebirgsschützenkorps*, Miesbach 1927.

Fiebig, E., *Husaren Heraus!*, Berlin 1933.

Förster, G., Hoch, P. & Müller, R., *Uniformen Europäischer Armeen*, East Berlin 1978.

Friese, Ulf-J. & Lacina, Uwe, *Die grauen Felduniformen der Deutschen Armee*, Hamburg, Reprint, Verlag Ruhl, Leipzig, n.d.

Gay, A. & Fiedler, S., *Die Grenadiermützen Friedrichs des Grossen*, Munich 1981.

Gesellschaft für Heereskunde, *Zeitschrift für Heereskunde*, Berlin 1929ff., official journal of the Deutsche Gesellschaft für Heereskunde, Berlin.

Gohlke, W., *Geschichte der gesammelten Feuerwaffen bis 1850 (1914)*, Reprint Krefeld 1977.

Gräfe Brothers, *Die Deutschen Helme vor Ausbruch des I. Weltkrieges*, Emmendingen 1970.

von Gritzner, M., *Ritter- und Verdienstorden*, Leipzig 1893, Reprint 1962.

Harell, John L., *Regimental Steins*, Frederick, Maryland USA 1979.

Hauthal, Dr. Ferdinand, *Geschichte der Sächsischen Armee*, Leipzig 1859.

Helm und Ströbel, *Die Feldgraue Friedensund Kriegsbekleidung der Königlichen Bayerischen Armee*, Munich 1916.

Henneking, G. & Koch, W., *Die Uniform des deutschen Eisenbahners*, Freiburg 1980.

Hermes, Sabina & Niemeyer, Joachim, *Altbadisches Militär von der Vereinigung der Markgrafschaften bis zur Reichsgründung 1771-1871*, Museum Schloss Rastatt, 1984.

von Hessenthal, Edler & Schreiber, G., *Die Ehrenzeichen des Deutschen Reiches*, Berlin 1940.

Hiltl & Schindler, *Preussens Heer unter Kaiser Wilhelm I*, Berlin 1856.

Huber, Dr. P. Engelbert, *Marie Gabrielle Prinzessin von Bayern*, Diessen vor München, 1914.

Hübener, Frank, *Reservistenkrüge und Reservistenpfeifen*, Munich 1982.

von Ilsemann, Sigurd, *Der Kaiser in Holland, Aufzeichnungen des letzten Flügeladjutanten Kaiser Wilhelms II, aus Amerongen und Doorn 1918-1941*, Munich 1967-68, 2 Vol.

Jany, Curt, *Geschichte der Preussischen Armee vom 15. Jahrhundert bis 1914, 6 Vol*, Osnabrück 1967.

Käuffer, *Geschichte des königlichen bayerischen 9. Infanterie-Regiments Wrede von seinem Ursprung bis zur Gegenwart*, Würzburg 1895.

Kersten, Fritz & Ortenburg, Georg, *Hessisches Militär zur Zeit des Deutschen Bundes*, Beckum 1984.

—*Die Sächsische Armee von 1763 bis 1862*, Beckum 1982.

Kling, C., *Geschichte der Bekleidung, Bewaffnung und Ausrüstung des Königlichen Preussischen Heeres, 3 Vol*, Weimar 1912.

Knötel, Herbert & Jantke, Pietsch, Collas, *Das Deutsche Heer, Friedensuniformen bei Ausbruch des Weltkrieges, 4 Text & Table Vol*, Hamburg 1935.

Knötel, Richard, *Mitteilungen zur Geschichte der militärischen Tracht*, Rathenow 1892-1921, Reprint 1980.

—*Handbuch der Uniformkunde*, Leipzig 1896.

Knötel, Richard, Vogt, Hermann & Lohmeyer, Julius, *Das Militärbilderbuch, Die Armeen Europas*, Glogau, n.d., Reprint 1979.

Knötel, Sieg H., *Farbiges Handbuch der Uniformkunde, Die Entwicklung der militärischen Tracht der deutschen Staaten, Osterreich-Ungarns*, Stuttgart 1985.

Koenig, Otto, *Kultur und Verhaltensforschung*, Deutscher Taschenbuchverlag 1970.

Krickel, G & Lange, G., *Das Deutsche Reichsheer*, Berlin 1892.

von Kries, A., *Geschichte des Königlichen Preussischen Kaiser Alexander Garde-Grenadier Regiments No. 1*, Berlin 1889.

Kube, Jan K., *Militaria der deutschen Kaiserzeit, Helme und Uniformen 1871-1914*, Munich 1977.

Kürschner, J., *Armee und Marine, ein Handbuch*, Braunschweig 1902.

Lainé, Didier, *L'Armée Allemande en 1914, Das Deutsche Heer/The German Army*, Paris 1984.

Lezius, Martin, *Das Ehrenkleid des Soldaten*, Berlin 1936.

Martin, Dr. Paul, *Der Bunte Rock*, Stuttgart 1969.

von Menzel, Adolph, *Die Armee Friedrichs des Grossen in ihrer Uniformierung*, Berlin 1908, Reprint Stuttgart-Munich 1978.

Měricka, Václâv, *Orden und Auszeichnungen*, Prague 1966.

—*Orden und Ehrenzeichen der Österreichischen-Ungarischen Monarchie*, Vienna 1974.

—*Das Buch der Orden und Auszeichnungen*, Prague 1966.

Mollo, John, *Die Bunte Welt der Uniform*, London-Stuttgart 1972.

Müller, H. & Kunter, H., *Europäische Helme*, East Berlin 1971.

Münich, Friedrich, *Geschichte der Entwicklung der bayerischen Armee seit zwei Jahrhunderten (1618-1870)*, Munich 1864.

Neppel von Nagyrévi, Georg, *Husaren in der Weltgeschichte*, Wiesbaden 1975 (Hungarian original edition 1973).

Niemann, Alfred, *Kaiser und Revolution*, Berlin 1928.

Olmes, J., *Das Sponton*, Vols. 1955 ff, Krefeld 1955 ff.

Ortenburg, G., *Mit Gott für König und Vaterland, Das Preussische Heer 1807-1914*, Munich 1978.

von der Osten-Sacken und Casberg, Paul, *Deutschlands Armee in feldgrauer Kriegs- und Friedensuniform*, Berlin 1916.

Pelet-Narbonne, K. H., *Geschichte der Brandenburg-Preussischen Reiterei*, Berlin 1905.

Perrot, A. M., *Historische Sammlung aller noch bestehenden Ritterorden der verschiedenen Nationen*, Leipzig 1821, Reprint Dortmund 1980.

von Pfannenberg, Leo, *Geschichte der Schloss-Garde-Kompanie Seiner Majestät des Kaisers und Königs 1829-1909*, Berlin 1909.

Pietsch, Paul, *Formationsund Uniformierungsgeschichte des Preussischen Heeres 1808-1914*, Berlin 1912 and Hamburg 1963-66, 2 Vol.

(Prussia) *Bekleidungsvorschrift für die Offiziere, Sanitätsoffiziere und Beamten des Königlichen Preussischen Heeres*, Berlin 1911.

—*Bekleidungs-Ordnung*, Berlin 1911.

—*Das Königliche Zeughaus, Amtlicher Führer*, Berlin 1914.

—*Rangliste der Königlichen Preussischen Armee und des XIII. (königlichen württembergischen) Armeekorps*, Berlin, various years.

—*Königlich preussische Armee*, Uniforms Abzeichen 1817.

—*Vollständige Dienstaltersliste der Offiziere der Königlichen Preussischen Armee, des XIII (königlichen württembergischen) Armeekorps und der kaiserlichen Schutztruppen mit Angabe des Datums der Patente zu den früheren Dienstgraden, nach den verschiedenen Waffengattungen zusammengestellt*, various years.

Prömper, Ingo, *Das Königliche Preussische Heer (1861-1865) in seiner gegenwärtigen Uniformierung, zusammengestellt und herausgegeben von F. W. Hammer, Tafeln gezeichnet von A. von Werner und R. Meinhardt*, Berlin 1862-1865, Verlag Beckum 1980.

Rabe, Edmund, Burger, Ludwig & Ortenburg, Georg, *Die Brandenburg-Preussische Armee in historischer Darstellung*, Beckum 1977.

Radecke, Erich, *Geschichte des Polizei-Tschakos, von der Alten Armee zur Polizei*, Hilden 1981.

Rankin, Robert H., *Helmets and Headdress of the Imperial German Army 1870-1918*, New Milford 1965.

Rascher, F., *Archiv für Waffen- und Uniformkunde, Illustrierte Zeitschrift für Forscher und Sammler*, Frankfurt 1918-1919.

Rattelmüller, Paul Ernst, *Das Bayerische Bürgermilitär*, Munich 1969.

von Rivier, Horst, *Die Mützenbänder, der Kaiserlich-Deutschen Marine 1848-1920*, Kolbermoor 1980.

Ruhl, Moritz (Publishers), *Die Uniform der Deutschen Armee, I. und II. Abteilung*, Leipzig 1914.

—*Die Graue Felduniform der Deutschen Armee*, 1910.

—*Die Uniformen der Deutschen Marine*, 1878, also 1907.

—*Die deutschen Schutztruppen in Afrika*, 1899 ff.

—*Die neue Deutsche Reichswehr*, 1919.

(Sachsen) *Rangliste der Königlich Sächsischen Armee*, Dresden, various years.

Schulz, Hugo F. W., *Die Preussischen Kavallerie-Regimenter 1913-14, Nach dem Gesetz vom 3. Juli 1913*, Friedberg 1985.

—*Die Bayerischen, Sächsischen und Württembergischen Kavallerie-Regimenter*, Friedeberg 1986.

Schwarze, Wolfgang, *Die Uniformen der Preussischen Garde von ihrer Entstehung 1704 bis 1836*, Wuppertal 1975.

von Schwertfeger-Volkmann, *Die Deutsche Soldatenkunde, 2 Vol*, Leipzig 1937.

von Seeger, Karl, *Marschallstab und Kesselpauke, Tradition und Brauchtum in der deutschen und österreichisch-ungarischen Armee*, Stuttgart 1937.

Sendtner, Kurt, *Rupprecht von Wittelsbach Kronprinz von Bayern*, Munich 1954.

von Stadlinger, I. J., *Geschichte des Württembergischen Kriegswesens*, Stuttgart 1856.

Staudinger, Karl, *Geschichte des Bayerischen Heeres 1651-1918, 8 Vol*, Munich 1901-1927.

Sturm Zigarettenbilderalbum, *Deutsche Uniformen, Zeitalter Deutsche Freiheitskriege*, Berlin 1934.

Teutsch, Bernhard von Lerchenfeld, *Deutschlands Wehr zu Lande und zur See*, Leipzig 1903.

von Toeche-Mittler, *Armee-Märsche, 3 Vol*, Neckargemünd 1975.

Transfeldt, von Brand & Quenstedt, *Wort und Brauch im deutschen Heer*, Hamburg 1967.

Trost, L. J., *Die Ritter- und Verdienst-Orden, Ehrenzeichen und Medaillen aller Souveräne und Staaten*, Vienna/Leipzig 1910.

Vollmer, Udo, *Die Armee des Königreichs Hannover, Bewaffnung und Geschichte von 1803-1866*, Schwäbisch Hall 1978.

Weiss, Otto, *Feldgrau in Krieg und Frieden, Uniformtafeln nach der Kabinettsordre 1915*, Berlin 1916.

Whittle, Tyler, *Kaiser Wilhelm II, Biographie*, Munich 1977.

Wohlfeil, Rainer & Dollinger, Hans, *Die Deutsche Reichswehr*, Wiesbaden 1977.

Zentner, Rolf-L., *Deutsche Militärhelme 1895-1975*, Bonn 1980.

von Zeppelin, C., *Die Heere und Flotten der Gegenwart, Deutschland*, Berlin 1896.

Zienert, J., *Unsere Marine-Uniform*, Hamburg 1971.

Zinnfigurenmuseum, *Deutsches, Kulmbach, Plassenburg*, Publications 1939 ff.

SCHIFFER ● MILITARY ● HISTORY

The Cavalry Regiments of Frederick the Great, 1756-1763 by Günter Dorn and Joachim Engelmann. A large format, color volume about Frederick's cavalry regiments. All cuirassier, dragoon and hussar regiments are illustrated with two color pages for each regiment and informative text including the history of their formation to their dissolution.

Size: 9" x 12"

160 pp.

70 color illustrations

1 map

ISBN: 0-88740-164-3   hard cover

$95.00

The Infantry Regiments of Frederick the Great, 1756-1763 Günter Dorn and Joachim Engelmann. The most famous field regiments and garrison regiments of Frederick's army documented in a splendid, large volume. Impressive color drawings and informative text. Regimental chronicles, lists of regimental commanders, etc.

Size: 9" x 12"

160 pp.

73 color illustrations

ISBN: 0-88740-163-5   hard cover

$95.00

GERMAN UNIFORMS OF THE 20TH CENTURY-VOLUME 1

German Uniforms of the 20th Century-Volume 1-Uniforms of the Panzer Troops-1917 to the Present Jörg M. Hormann. This book covers the uniforms, insignias and emblems of the German tank troops from their formation towards the end of WWI to the present. This great variety of material is presented in many color and black and white photographs and explanatory remarks.

Size: 6" x 9"   126 pp.
Over 200 photographs
ISBN: 0-88740-214-3   hard cover $24.95

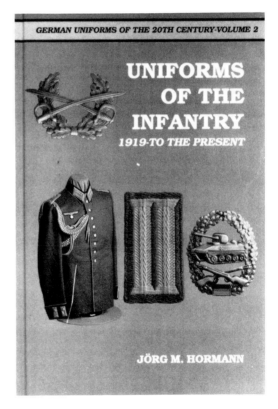

German Uniforms of the 20th Century-Volume 2-Uniforms of the Infantry-1919 to the Present Jörg M. Hormann. Along with its companion, Volume 1, this volume on infantry uniforms gives an in depth study to this often neglected area of military interest. Both books are ideal for collectors and hobbyists.

Size: 6" x 9"   126 pp.
Over 200 photographs
ISBN:0-88740-215-1 hardcover $24.95

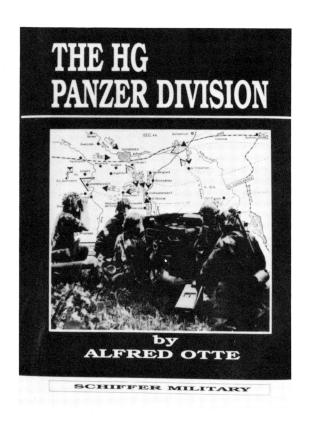

The HG Panzer Division Alfred Otte. This panzer division was formed from the Luftwaffe and took the name of its commander-in-chief, Herman Göring. It was originally formed as a motorized police unit, however, it later became a panzer regiment and eventually expanded to divisional size. The HG Panzer Division fought in the African Campaign, the Italian Campaign, on the eastern and western fronts and in the final defense of Germany. This is their story.

Size: 7 3/4" x 10 1/2"   176 pp.
325 b/w photographs, maps, documents
ISBN: 0-88740-206-2   hard cover
$24.95

•DIVISIONAL HISTORIES•

The Waffen-SS Herbert Walther. This fascinating pictorial and factual documentation presents the history of the Waffen-SS from their initial formation to the end of the war. Over 500 photographs, many taken in the heat of battle, show the Waffen-SS divisions on many fronts, in victory and in defeat. This book explains in words and pictures the development of the Waffen-SS and their place in modern history.

Size: 7 3/4" x 10 1/2"   240 pp.
500+ b/w photographs
ISBN: 0-88740-204-6   hard cover
$24.95

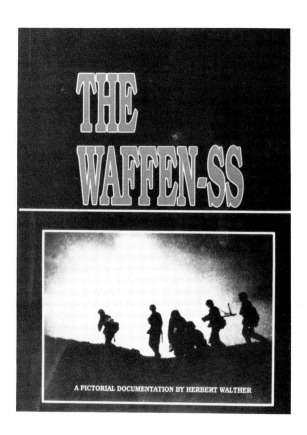